The
Wiersbe
BIBLE STUDY SERIES

1 SAMUEL

Attaining

Wealth

That Money

Can't Buy

David C Cook®

transforming lives together

THE WIERSBE BIBLE STUDY SERIES: 1 SAMUEL
Published by David C Cook
4050 Lee Vance View
Colorado Springs, CO 80918 U.S.A.

David C Cook Distribution Canada
55 Woodslee Avenue, Paris, Ontario, Canada N3L 3E5

David C Cook U.K., Kingsway Communications
Eastbourne, East Sussex BN23 6NT, England

The graphic circle C logo is a registered trademark of David C Cook.

All Scripture quotations in this study are taken from the Holy Bible, New
International Version®, NIV®. Copyright © 1973, 1984 by Biblica, Inc.™ Used by
permission of Zondervan. All rights reserved worldwide. www.zondervan.com.

In the *Be Successful* excerpts, unless otherwise noted, all Scripture quotations are taken
from the King James Version of the Bible. (Public Domain.) Scripture quotations marked
NIV are taken from the Holy Bible, New International Version®. NIV®. Copyright © 1973,
1978, 1984 by International Bible Society. Used by permission of Zondervan. All rights
reserved; NASB are taken from the New American Standard Bible, © Copyright 1960, 1995
by The Lockman Foundation. Used by permission; NKJV are taken from the New King
James Version. Copyright © 1982 by Thomas Nelson, Inc. Used by permission. All rights
reserved; and NLT are taken from the New Living Translation of the Holy Bible. New Living
Translation copyright © 1996, 2004 by Tyndale Charitable Trust. Used by permission of
Tyndale House Publishers. All excerpts taken from *Be Successful*, second edition, published
by David C Cook in 2010 © 2001 Warren W. Wiersbe, ISBN 978-1-4347-6500-0.

LCCN 2013941280
ISBN 978-1-4347-0505-1
eISBN 978-0-7814-1083-0

© 2013 Warren W. Wiersbe

The Team: Steve Parolini, Karen Lee-Thorp, Amy Konyndyk,
Nick Lee, Tonya Osterhouse, Karen Athen
Series Cover Design: John Hamilton Design
Cover Photo: iStockphoto

Printed in the United States of America

First Edition 2013

1 2 3 4 5 6 7 8 9 10

080113

The
Wiersbe
BIBLE STUDY SERIES

Contents

Introduction to 1 Samuel

Success Story

Some say success is simply achieving your goals, but how do we know those goals were worth achieving? Are you a success if you reach contemptible goals by dishonorable means? Adolf Hitler had a frightening definition of success: "the sole and earthly judge of right and wrong." In short, might makes right.

First Samuel is a book about success and failure, both in individuals and in a nation. The nation of Israel failed. Eli and his sons were failures. King Saul started out a success but soon became a failure. David was a success in his character, conduct, and service. He was a man after God's own heart.

The Value of Value

"Try not to become a man of success," wrote Albert Einstein, "but rather try to become a man of value." Values involve character, which is why Theodore Roosevelt said, "The chief factor in any man's success or failure must be his own character." Eli, the priest, and Saul, the king, both had reputations; but David had character. His character and skills were developed in private before they were demonstrated in public.

Until individuals, churches, and nations start emphasizing character and obedience, there can never be true success. Only through faith in Jesus Christ and obedience to His will can we have godly character and the kind of success that will survive the fires of God's judgment.

—*Warren W. Wiersbe*

How to Use This Study

This study is designed for both individual and small-group use. We've divided it into eight lessons—each references one or more chapters in Warren W. Wiersbe's commentary *Be Successful* (second edition, David C Cook, 2010). While reading *Be Successful* is not a prerequisite for going through this study, the additional insights and background Wiersbe offers can greatly enhance your study experience.

The **Getting Started** questions at the beginning of each lesson offer you an opportunity to record your first thoughts and reactions to the study text. This is an important step in the study process as those "first impressions" often include clues about what it is your heart is longing to discover.

The bulk of the study is found in the **Going Deeper** questions. These dive into the Bible text and, along with helpful excerpts from Wiersbe's commentary, help you examine not only the original context and meaning of the verses but also modern application.

Looking Inward narrows the focus down to your personal story. These intimate questions can be a bit uncomfortable at times, but don't shy away from honesty here. This is where you are asked to stand before the mirror of God's Word and look closely at what you see. It's the place to take a good look at yourself in light of the lesson and search for ways in which you can grow in faith.

Going Forward is the place where you can commit to paper those things you want or need to do in order to better live out the discoveries you made in the Looking Inward section. Don't skip or skim through this. Take the time to really consider what practical steps you might take to move closer to Christ. Then share your thoughts with a trusted friend who can act as an encourager and accountability partner.

Finally, there is a brief **Seeking Help** section to close the lesson. This is a reminder for you to invite God into your spiritual-growth process. If you choose to write out a prayer in this section, come back to it as you work through the lesson and continue to seek the Holy Spirit's guidance as you discover God's will for your life.

Tips for Small Groups

A small group is a dynamic thing. One week it might seem like a group of close-knit friends. The next it might seem more like a group of uncomfortable strangers. A small-group leader's role is to read these subtle changes and adjust the tone of the discussion accordingly.

Small groups need to be safe places for people to talk openly. It is through shared wrestling with difficult life issues that some of the greatest personal growth is discovered. But in order for the group to feel safe, participants need to know it's okay *not* to share sometimes. Always invite honest disclosure, but never force someone to speak if he or she isn't comfortable doing so. (A savvy leader will follow up later with a group member who isn't comfortable sharing in a group setting to see if a one-on-one discussion is more appropriate.)

Have volunteers take turns reading excerpts from Scripture or from the commentary. The more each person is involved even in the mundane tasks, the more they'll feel comfortable opening up in more meaningful ways.

The leader should watch the clock and keep the discussion moving. Sometimes there may be more Going Deeper questions than your group can cover in your available time. If you've had a fruitful discussion, it's okay to move on without finishing everything. And if you think the group is getting bogged down on a question or has taken off on a tangent, you can simply say, "Let's go on to question 5." Be sure to save at least ten to fifteen minutes for the Going Forward questions.

Finally, soak your group meetings in prayer—before you begin, during as needed, and always at the end of your time together.

Lord of Hosts
(1 SAMUEL 1—3)

Before you begin ...
- *Pray for the Holy Spirit to reveal truth and wisdom as you go through this lesson.*
- *Read 1 Samuel 1—3. This lesson references chapter 1, "'The Lord of Hosts Is with Us,'" in* Be Successful. *It will be helpful for you to have your Bible and a copy of the commentary available as you work through this lesson.*

Getting Started

From the Commentary

The story of the people of Israel recorded in the Bible is a living demonstration of the fact that the Lord *does* win the battle, that He is sovereign in all things. People and events recorded in Scripture are part of what theologians call "salvation history," God's gracious plan to send the Savior into the world to die for sinners. The book of Ruth ends with the name of David (Ruth 4:22), and 1 Samuel tells the story of David's successful preparation for reigning on the throne of Israel. It was from David's family that Jesus Christ, the "son of David," was born. The books of Samuel, Kings, and Chronicles record many sins and failures on the part of God's people, but they also remind us that God is on the throne, and when He isn't allowed to rule, He overrules. He is the Lord of Hosts, and His purposes will be accomplished.

—*Be Successful*, page 16

1. Why would God choose to include a book such as 1 Samuel in the Bible? What is it about the successes and failures that He wants His people to learn from? David is given plenty of attention in this book. What makes him such a compelling character in the biblical narrative?

More to Consider: During the dark days of the Judges, a love story took place that's recorded in the book of Ruth. Boaz married Ruth the Moabitess, and from their union came Obed, the father of Jesse, who became the father of David the king. If Judges is the book of "no king," then in what ways is 1 Samuel the book of "man's king"? Why did the people of Israel so desperately desire a king? How did that work out?

2. Choose one verse or phrase from 1 Samuel 1—3 that stands out to you. This could be something you're intrigued by, something that makes you uncomfortable, something that puzzles you, something that resonates with you, or just something you want to examine further. Write that here.

Going Deeper

From the Commentary

Samuel was God's "bridge builder" at a critical time in Jewish history when the weak confederation of tribes desperately needed direction. He was the last of the judges (1 Sam. 7:15–17; Acts 13:20) and the first of a new line of prophets after Moses (3:24). He established a school of the prophets, and he anointed two kings—Saul who failed and David who succeeded. At a time when the ages were colliding and everything seemed to be shaking, Samuel gave spiritual leadership to the nation of Israel and helped to move them toward national unification and spiritual rededication.

In human history, it may appear to us that truth is "forever on the scaffold" and wrong is "forever on the throne," but that isn't heaven's point of view. As you study 1 Samuel, you will see clearly that God is always in control. While He is long-suffering and merciful and answers the prayers of His people, He is also holy and just and punishes sin. We live today in a time of radical worldwide change, and the church needs leaders like Samuel who will help God's people understand where they've been, who they are, and what they are called to do.

What an example Hannah is in her praying! It was a prayer born out of sorrow and suffering, but in spite of her feelings, she laid bare her soul before the Lord. It was a prayer that involved submission, for she presented herself to the Lord as His handmaiden, to do whatever He wanted her to do (see Luke 1:48). It was a prayer that also involved sacrifice, because she vowed to give her son back to the Lord, to be a Nazirite (Num. 6) and serve the Lord all his life. In praying like this, was Hannah "bargaining" with the Lord? I don't think so. Bearing a son would have removed her disgrace and perhaps ended her rival's persecution, but giving up the son was another matter. Perhaps it would have been easier for her to go on living in barrenness than to have a child for three years and have to give him up forever. I wonder if God had given Hannah an inner conviction that her son would play an important part in the future of the nation.

—Be Successful, pages 17–20

3. Respond to this quote: "In human history, it may appear to us that truth is 'forever on the scaffold' and wrong is 'forever on the throne.'" Why might people believe this is true? How does 1 Samuel support this idea? How does it challenge the idea?

From the Commentary

During the period of the judges, the Israelites were in dire straits because they lacked godly leadership. The priesthood was defiled, there was no sustained prophetic message from the Lord (3:1), and the law of Moses was being ignored throughout the land. As He often did in Israel's history, God began to solve the problem by sending a baby. Babies are God's announcement that He knows the need, cares about His people, and is at work on their behalf. The arrival of a baby ushers in new life and a new beginning; babies are signposts to the future, and their conception and birth is a miracle that only God can do (Gen. 30:1–2). To make the event seem even greater, God sometimes selects barren women to be the mothers, as when He sent Isaac to Sarah, Jacob and Esau to Rebekah, and Joseph to Rachel.

—*Be Successful*, page 18

4. Review 1 Samuel 1:1–28. Why would God choose to send His "new beginnings" in the form of an infant? What message does this give us about how God's mind works? About His patience? About His love for His creation? About His plan for redemption?

From the Commentary

"What are all histories but God manifesting Himself," said Oliver Cromwell over three centuries ago, but not everybody agrees with him. The British historian Edward Gibbon, who wrote *The Decline and Fall of the Roman Empire*, called history "little more than the register of crimes, follies, and misfortunes of mankind," and Lord Chesterfield, his contemporary, called history "a confused heap of facts." But Dr. A. T. Pierson, preacher and missionary statesman of the last century, said it best when he wrote, "History is His story."

—*Be Successful*, page 16

5. In what ways is all of history "God's story"? How does this perspective change the way we view history? How do we reconcile the darker parts of history with God's plan? Where do we see God at work in the best and worst aspects of our history, not just in America, but globally?

From the Commentary

When Elkanah and Hannah presented their son to the Lord, Hannah reminded Eli that she was the woman who had prayed for a son three years before. Did the old man remember the occasion, and did he recall how unfairly he had dealt with this sorrowing woman? If he did, there's no record of it, but he received the boy to become a servant of the Lord at the tabernacle and be trained in the Law of the Lord.

Considering the low level of spiritual life in Eli and the

wicked ways of his sons, it took a great deal of faith for Elkanah and Hannah to leave their innocent son in their care. But the Lord was with Samuel and would preserve him from the pollution around him. Just as God protected Joseph in Egypt, so He would protect Samuel in Shiloh, and so He can protect our children and grandchildren in this present evil world. Judgment was coming to Eli and his family, but God would have Samuel prepared to guide the nation and move them into the next stage of their development.

—*Be Successful*, pages 22–23

6. In what ways does Samuel's story make it clear that the life and future of a nation depends on the character of the home? How does the following quote from Confucius relate to this concept: "The strength of a nation is derived from the integrity of its homes"? How does Samuel's story speak to the power of a little child dedicated to God? What message can we take from this regarding how we raise our children today?

From the Commentary

After Hannah left her son with Eli, she could have gone off alone and had a good cry, but instead she burst into a song of praise to the Lord. The world doesn't understand the relationship between sacrifice and song, how God's people can sing their way into sacrifice and sacrifice their way into singing. "And when the burnt offering began, the song of the Lord began also" (2 Chron. 29:27). Before He went to the garden where He would be arrested, Jesus sang a hymn with His disciples (Matt. 26:30), and Paul and Silas sang hymns to the Lord after they had been humiliated and beaten (Acts 16:20–26). Frequently in the psalms you find David praising God in the midst of difficult circumstances. After being beaten by the religious leaders in Jerusalem, the apostles "departed from the presence of the council, rejoicing that they were counted worthy to suffer shame for His name" (Acts 5:41 NKJV).

—*Be Successful*, pages 23–24

7. Compare Hannah's song near the beginning of 1 Samuel to David's song found near the end of 2 Samuel (chap. 22), as well as to Mary's song in Luke 1:46–55. How are they similar? How are they different? What does each of the songs reveal about God's presence in these people's lives?

From the Commentary

> It's good for us to begin our praying with praising, because
> praise helps us focus on the glory of the Lord and not on
> the greatness of our needs. When we see the greatness of
> God, we start to see life in perspective. Hannah knew
> the character of God and exalted His glorious attributes.
> She began by affirming His *holiness* and *uniqueness*. The
> two go together because in both Hebrew and Greek the
> word "holy" means "wholly other, set apart, separated."
> Orthodox Jews confess daily, "Hear, O Israel: The Lord
> our God is one Lord" (Deut. 6:4). There is no other God,
> and whenever Israel turned to idols for help, they lost the
> blessing of the Lord.
>
> —*Be Successful*, page 25

8. The "Rock" is one of the repeated images of the Lord in the Scriptures. Read Deuteronomy 32:4, 15, 18, 30–31, 37 and 2 Samuel 22:32. What does *Rock* convey about God in these passages? How does that compare to its use in 1 Samuel 2:2?

More to Consider: Hannah rejoiced because this holy God is a just judge of the actions of His people. Unlike the people involved in human judicial proceedings, the Lord knows everything and is able to weigh us and our actions accurately. Read Daniel 5:27 and Proverbs 16:2; 24:11–12. What does each of these passages tell us about God's role as judge? Why is God's justice so important to His people?

From the Commentary

Up to this point, the focus has been on Elkanah and his family (1:1—2:11), but now it will shift to Eli and his family (2:12—3:21). Throughout this section, you will see a deliberate contrast between Samuel and the two sons of Eli, Hophni and Phinehas. Eli's sons "abhorred the offering of the Lord" (2:17), but "Samuel ministered before the Lord" (v. 18). The two brothers committed evil deeds at the tabernacle and invited God's judgment, but Samuel served at the tabernacle and grew in God's favor (v. 26). The priestly line would end in Eli's family, but Samuel would be called of God to carry on a holy priesthood (2:34—3:1).

—*Be Successful*, pages 27–28

9. Review 1 Samuel 2:12–36. In what ways does it appear as though Eli's evil sons got away with their disobedience? How is this like the way we sometimes view people's actions today? How was God actually preparing judgment for them during this time? How was God also preparing Samuel for his great work?

From the Commentary

Once again we see the contrast between the wickedness of Eli's family and the faithfulness of the boy Samuel (v. 1). He ministered before the Lord under the guidance of Eli at a time when God wasn't speaking to His people very often. The spiritual leaders were corrupt, and God's people weren't obeying His law anyway, so why should God say anything new to them? It was a tragic day in the nation of Israel when the living God no longer sent His people signs and prophetic messages (Ps. 74:9; Ezek. 7:26; Amos 8:11–12; Mic. 3:6). The silence of God was the judgment of God.

—*Be Successful*, pages 31–32

10. Review 1 Samuel 3:1–21. In what ways was God's silence His judgment? What was God about to do to change the situation? How does God once again use a young child to spark a change in His people?

Looking Inward

Take a moment to reflect on all that you've explored thus far in this study of 1 Samuel 1—3. Review your notes and answers and think about how each of these things matters in your life today.

> *Tips for Small Groups: To get the most out of this section, form pairs or trios and have group members take turns answering these questions. Be honest and as open as you can in this discussion, but most of all, be encouraging and supportive of others. Be sensitive to those who are going through particularly difficult times and don't press for people to speak if they're uncomfortable doing so.*

11. God often introduces His agent of change as an infant. How does this make you feel? Does God's creative investment in babies and children affect the way you relate to them? What message does it give you about how to treat children? About trusting God even when things look dire?

12. In what ways is God your Rock? What does confidence in God look like to you? How do you go about building your confidence in God?

13. Think about the last time you observed someone getting away with something. Where was God during that circumstance? What are some ways you've seen God use other people's apparent evil for good? How has God used your own sins to grow your faith?

Going Forward

14. Think of one or two things that you have learned that you'd like to work on in the coming week. Remember that this is all about quality, not quantity. It's better to work on one specific area of life and do it well than to work on many and do poorly (or to be so overwhelmed that you simply don't try).

Do you want to pursue greater confidence in God as your Rock? Be specific. Go back through 1 Samuel 1—3 and put a star next to the phrase or verse that is most encouraging to you. Consider memorizing this verse.

Real-Life Application Ideas: Hannah remained strong in the midst of difficult circumstances. She learned how to suffer in a godly way. This week, focus on practical ways you can lean more on God in those areas where you're experiencing disappointment or pain. Study Scripture passages that offer encouragement and hope. Then share all you've learned with someone who is going through a particularly difficult time.

Seeking Help

15. Write a prayer below (or simply pray one in silence), inviting God to work on your mind and heart in those areas you've noted in the Going Forward section. Be honest about your desires and fears.

Notes for Small Groups:

- *Look for ways to put into practice the things you wrote in the Going Forward section. Talk with other group members about your ideas and commit to being accountable to one another.*

- *During the coming week, ask the Holy Spirit to continue to reveal truth to you from what you've read and studied.*

- *Before you start the next lesson, read 1 Samuel 4—11. For more in-depth lesson preparation, read chapters 2, "Israel's Defeat—God's victory," and 3, "The Call for a King," in* Be Successful.

Defeat and Victory
(1 SAMUEL 4—11)

Before you begin ...
- *Pray for the Holy Spirit to reveal truth and wisdom as you go through this lesson.*
- *Read 1 Samuel 4—11. This lesson references chapters 2 and 3 in* Be Successful. *It will be helpful for you to have your Bible and a copy of the commentary available as you work through this lesson.*

Getting Started

From the Commentary

The ark of the covenant is mentioned at least thirty-five times in chapters 4—6 and represents Jehovah God, the central Person in all of Israel's history. The ark was the most important piece of furniture in the tabernacle and resided in the Holy of Holies. In the ark were the two tablets of the law, and on it was the golden "mercy seat" where God's glorious presence dwelt. This was the throne of God from which He spoke to His people (Ex. 25:10–22).

—*Be Successful,* page 37

1. Why was it important to have a physical manifestation or symbol of God's presence in ancient times? What does this say about the people's relationship with their God? How was the ark of the covenant a part of God's bigger plan to chasten His people, judge sinners, and eventually establish His anointed king?

More to Consider: The Philistines are mentioned in Scripture as early as the days of Abraham (Gen. 21:32), and in the books of Samuel they're mentioned over 150 times. They were originally a seagoing people from the Aegean region who invaded the territory along the Mediterranean coast (Phoenicia) and sought to control all of the land we know as Palestine. Do some research on the Philistines. Why did they try to drive the Israelites out of the Promised Land so many times? How did the constant threat of invasion affect the lives of God's people? What lessons did God teach through these trying circumstances?

2. Choose one verse or phrase from 1 Samuel 4—11 that stands out to you. This could be something you're intrigued by, something that makes you uncomfortable, something that puzzles you, something that resonates with you, or just something you want to examine further. Write that here.

Going Deeper

From the Commentary

The five key cities of the Philistines were Ashdod, Gaza, Ashkelon, Gath, and Ekron, and each had a ruler or "lord" (6:16–17). The Philistines first put the ark into the temple of their god Dagon in Ashdod as evidence that Dagon was stronger and greater than Jehovah. At the beginning of the battle, the Philistines were frightened when they heard that the God of Israel was in the camp, but now they were making fun of Him and exalting their own gods. In their mythology, Dagon was the principal god of the Philistines and the father of Baal, the storm god, whose worship brought so much trouble to Israel.

However, Dagon didn't have a chance, for Jehovah God was and is well able to take care of Himself! The next morning, the worshippers found Dagon prostrate before the ark like one of the worshippers. Like every dead idol, Dagon had to be righted again (Ps. 115), but things were even worse the next morning. The stump of Dagon was prostrate before the ark of the covenant, but his head and hands had been cut off and placed at the threshold of the temple! But that wasn't the end, for the Lord not only humiliated the god of the Philistines, but He also judged the people who worshipped that god. When the Philistines captured the ark and arrogantly treated the Lord as though He were just another god, they invited the judgment of God.

When you put the evidence together, it seems that the Lord sent infected mice or rats (1 Sam. 6:4) among the people and spread a terrible plague. According to the covenant, the Lord should have sent this affliction on the unbelieving Jews (Deut. 28:58–60), but in His grace, He punished the enemy. Some students believe this was the bubonic plague and that the people experienced painful inflammatory swellings of the lymph glands, especially in the groin. Others think it was a plague of tumors, perhaps severe hemorrhoids (see 1 Sam. 5:9), although it's difficult to understand the part the rats played in this affliction.

—*Be Successful*, pages 41–42

3. Review 1 Samuel 5:1–12. Why did the Philistines attribute their circumstance to the presence of the ark? What does this say about their belief system? What does it say about God? Why was superstition such a big part of the ancient religions? How does it still play a role today?

From the Commentary

The experiences described in 1 Samuel 5:1–12 occurred during a period of seven months, at the end of which the five lords decided it was time to get rid of the ark. They wouldn't admit it, but Jehovah had vindicated Himself before the Philistines and humiliated their false god. Still wanting to save face, the lords sought some way to send the ark back to Israel without directly involving themselves or their people.

The Philistine wise men came up with a scheme that would test the God of Israel one more time. If Jehovah, represented by the ark, was indeed the true and living God, *let Him take the ark back to where it belonged*! The lords set up a plan that would absolve them of responsibility and blame. They would take two cows that had calves and separate them from the calves. They would hitch the cows to a new cart, put the ark on the cart, and turn the cows loose. If the cows didn't move at all, or if they went to their calves, it would be "proof" that the God of Israel wasn't in control and the Philistines had nothing to fear. If the cows meandered all over without any sense of direction, the lords could draw the same conclusion. The situation being what it was, the cows would probably head for their calves, because that was the natural thing to do. The cows needed to get rid of their milk and the calves needed the nourishment.

But that wasn't all. The wise men decided that the nation had to send "appeasement gifts" to Jehovah in the form of golden models of the mice and the tumors. If the cows didn't head for Israelite territory, the Philistines could always reclaim their gold. If the cows went over the border into Israel, the Lord would be appeased and wouldn't send Philistia any more plagues. This plan enabled the Lord to receive glory without the lords of the Philistines being embarrassed. When you consider that the cows were nursing their calves and lowing for them, and that the cows had never drawn a cart before, the odds were that they wouldn't go down the road that led from Ekron to Beth-Shemesh. The five lords and their wise men had it all figured out.

But they were wrong. The lords of the Philistines didn't know the true and living God, but the cows did, and they obeyed Him! "The ox knows its owner and the donkey its master's crib" (Isa. 1:3 NKJV). They crossed the border and came to the priestly city of Beth-Shemesh (Josh. 21:13–16) where the men were working in the fields harvesting the wheat. They joyfully welcomed the return of the ark, and the Levites took it off the cart and put it on a great stone in the field.

Grateful that the throne of God had been restored to His people, the Levites offered the cows as burnt offerings to the Lord, and in their joy ignored the fact that only male animals could legally be offered (Lev. 1:3). Other men from the city brought additional sacrifices. They also put the golden gifts on the rock and offered them to the Lord. Since Shiloh had been destroyed and there was no sanctuary available for worship, they used the large rock as an altar, and the Lord accepted their offerings. What the Lord is looking for is a broken and contrite heart, not a slavish obedience to the letter of the law (Ps. 51:15–17). The enemy was near at hand (1 Sam. 6:16), and the Jewish men didn't dare leave the place to which God had directed the cows.

—*Be Successful*, pages 43–44

4. Review 1 Samuel 6:1–18. What did God do with the cows what Dagon could never do? What does this tell us about God's creativity? What are similar stories from the Bible that reveal God's power over all of nature?

From the Commentary

The men of Beth-Shemesh should have covered the ark, because it wasn't supposed to be seen by anyone except the high priest, and this mistake was costly. Some of the people became curious and looked into the ark and were slain. If the pagan Philistines were judged for the way they treated the ark, how much more responsible were the Jews who knew the law and were living in a Levitical city!

Students have debated the accuracy of the number of people who were killed, because 50,000 seems too high for a town like Beth-Shemesh. Some make the number only 70 and say that the 50,000 is a scribal error, and perhaps it is. The Hebrews used letters for numbers, and it would be easy for a copyist to make a mistake. Others include in the 50,000 the 4,000 plus "the great slaughter" (4:17) on the battlefield, but the text specifically says it was the irreverent people who looked into the ark who were slain. (See 1 Sam. 6:19; Lev. 16:13; Num. 1:50–51; 4:5, 16–20.) It isn't likely that 50,000 people lined up and passed by the ark, for the people queued up would have scattered when the first viewers were killed. Perhaps they were slain later. Certainly the Levites would have protected the ark from the curious, for they knew the penalties for breaking the law of God. That 70 men were judged isn't difficult to believe, but 50,000 seems extravagant. However, since we don't know the population of Beth-Shemesh and its environs, we can't pass judgment on the text. One day an archeologist may solve the problem for us.

—*Be Successful*, page 45

5. Review 1 Samuel 6:19–20. Is the number of people who were slain an important detail in this story? Why or why not? What is the bottom line in all this? What was the lesson to be learned? Today God doesn't live in a physical place (see Acts 7:48–50). In light of that, what is the relevance of the story in 6:19–20 for us today? (See Heb. 10:31.)

From the Commentary

The Lord could have withdrawn Himself from His people, but instead, He graciously allowed the ark to be taken about ten miles to Kiriath Jearim where it remained in the home of Abinadab. The men of the city consecrated Abinadab's son Eleazar to guard the ark. This was undoubtedly a Levitical family, for after what had happened to the men of Beth-Shemesh, the men weren't likely to take any more chances by breaking the law! The ark remained in Kiriath Jearim for perhaps a century, for the battle of Aphek was fought about 1104 BC, and David brought the ark to Jerusalem in about 1003 BC (2 Sam. 6). The ark had been in the home of Abinadab twenty years when Samuel called an assembly of the people to turn from their sins and seek the Lord (1 Sam. 7:3).

The ark of the covenant represented the presence of the Lord with His people and the rule of the Lord over His people. The Lord had every right to abandon His sinful people, but He graciously remained with them, though not in the special tabernacle He had commanded them to build. It was a difficult time for the Jews, for they were not a united people, nor were they a godly people. Israel thought that their problems would be solved if they had a king like the other nations, but they would discover that having their own way would lead them into greater problems. God still gives His best to those who leave the choice with Him.

—Be Successful, page 46

6. How was the ark to Israel like Jesus is to God's people today? What lessons can we learn from the way the Israelites (and pagans) treated the ark that can inform our relationship with Jesus? (See 1 Peter 3:15.)

From the Commentary

Samuel discerned that the people were restless and wanting change, and he knew that times of transition bring out either the best or the worst in people. God called Samuel to build a bridge between the turbulent age of the judges and the new era of the monarchy, and it wasn't an easy task. There was one thing Samuel knew for certain: King or no king, the nation could never succeed if the people didn't put the Lord first and trust only in Him. That's why he called for a meeting at Mizpah, a city in Benjamin (Josh. 18:26), where he challenged God's covenant people to return to the Lord.

Idolatry had been Israel's besetting sin. Jacob's family carried false gods with them (Gen. 35:2), and when the Jews were slaves in Egypt, they adopted the gods and goddesses of the Egyptians, and after the exodus, worshipped some of these idols during the wilderness journeys (Acts

7:42–43). Moses commanded Israel to destroy every evidence of Canaanite religion, but the people eventually lapsed back into idolatry and worshipped the gods of the defeated enemy. Samuel specifically mentioned the Baals and Ashtoreths (1 Sam. 7:3–4). Baal was the Canaanite storm god to whom the Jews often turned when the land was suffering drought, and Ashtoreth was the goddess of fertility whose worship included unspeakably sensual activities. At Mount Sinai, the Jews didn't see a representation of God, but they heard His voice, and they knew that worshipping any image of their God was to practice false worship.

—Be Successful, pages 49–50

7. In what ways was putting away their false gods only the beginning of the Jews' return to the Lord? What else did they do to turn back toward Him? Why was it so important to give up idols first? How do idols get in the way?

More to Consider: The setting up of stones to commemorate significant events has been a part of the Hebrew culture since Jacob set up a memorial at Bethel (Gen. 28:20–22; 35:14). "Joshua set up twelve stones that had been in the middle of the Jordan" (Josh. 4:9) and twelve more on the western bank at Gilgal to mark the place where the waters opened and Israel crossed into the Promised Land (Josh. 4:1–8, 19–21). A great heap of stones in the Achor Valley reminded the Jews of Achan's disobedience (Josh. 7:24–26), and another heap marked the burial place of the king of Ai (8:29). Another heap stood at a cave at Makkedah to mark where five kings had been defeated and slain (10:25–27). Before his death, Joshua set up a "witness stone" to remind the Israelites of their vow to serve the Lord alone and obey Him (24:26–28). What did the stones represent in Samuel's story? What were they meant to remind the Israelites of? What are some of the "stones of remembrance" we have in our churches today?

From the Commentary

Probably twenty or twenty-five years elapsed between the events recorded in chapter 7 and those in chapter 8. Samuel was now an old man, about to pass from the scene, and a new generation had emerged in Israel with new leaders who had new ideas. Life goes on, circumstances change, and God's people must have wisdom to adapt to new challenges without abandoning old convictions. Like more than one great leader, Samuel in his old age faced some painful situations and had to make some difficult decisions. He left the scene convinced that he had been rejected by the people he had served so faithfully. Samuel obeyed the Lord, but he was a man with a broken heart.

God had chosen Moses to lead the nation of Israel and Joshua to succeed him (Deut. 31:1–15), but Joshua wasn't commanded to lay hands on any successor. He left behind elders he had trained to serve God, but when they died, the new generation turned away from the Lord and followed the idols of the land (Judg. 2:10–15). There was an automatic succession to the priesthood, and the Lord could call out prophets when needed, but who would lead the people and see to it that the law was obeyed? During the period of the judges, God raised up leaders here and there and gave them great victories, but nobody was in charge of the nation as a whole. "In those days there was no king in Israel; every man did that which was right in his own eyes" (Judg. 21:25; see 17:6; 18:1; 19:1). The "nation" of Israel was a loose confederation of sovereign tribes, and each tribe was expected to seek the Lord and do His will.

—*Be Successful*, pages 53–54

8. How was Samuel's situation unique in the history of God's people? How is his role similar to and different from leaders in the church today? Who chooses the leaders today? What role does God play directly? What role do God's people play?

From the Commentary

What's true of individuals is true of nations: You take what you want from life and you pay for it. Under the kingship of Jehovah God, the nation had security and sufficiency as long as they obeyed Him, and His demands were not unreasonable. To obey God's covenant meant to live a happy life as the Lord gave you all that you needed and more. But the key word in Samuel's speech is *take*, not give. The king and his court had to be supported, so he would take their sons and daughters, their property, their harvests, and their flocks and herds. Their choice young men would serve in the army as well as in the king's fields. Their daughters would cook and bake for the king. He would take their property and part of their harvest in order to feed the officials and servants in the royal household. While these things weren't too evident under Saul and David, they were certainly obvious under Solomon (1 Kings 4:7–28). The day came when the people cried out for relief from the heavy yoke Solomon had put on them just to maintain the glory of his kingdom (12:1–4; see Jer. 22:13–17).

—*Be Successful*, page 56

9. Why did the people insist that God give them a king? What was uppermost in their minds with this kind of thinking? What sorts of guarantees did they want from God?

From the Commentary

> One of the reasons Israel asked for a king was so the nation could unite behind one leader and have a better opportunity to face their enemies. The Lord condescended to reach down to their level of unbelief, and He gave them a king who looked like a natural warrior. How sad it is that God's people trusted a man of clay whom they could admire, and yet they would not trust the Lord who throughout the nation's history had proven Himself powerful on their behalf. In His grace, God gave Saul an opportunity to prove himself and consolidate his authority.
>
> —*Be Successful*, page 64

10. Review 1 Samuel 11:1–15. What opportunity did God give Saul to prove himself? What challenge did he face? What was the result of that challenge? How did this situation reveal Samuel's role as the Lord's servant?

Looking Inward

Take a moment to reflect on all that you've explored thus far in this study of 1 Samuel. Review your notes and answers and think about how each of these things matters in your life today.

> *Tips for Small Groups: To get the most out of this section, form pairs or trios and have group members take turns answering these questions. Be honest and as open as you can in this discussion, but most of all, be encouraging and supportive of others. Be sensitive to those who are going through particularly difficult times and don't press for people to speak if they're uncomfortable doing so.*

11. In the time of the Old Testament, God localized His presence on the ark of the covenant. Would you prefer to have lived during this time, when God's presence was specific and measurable? Why or why not? In what ways were the Israelites practicing a kind of "blind faith"? How does that faith compare to the faith you have today?

12. The Philistines hedged their bets when it came to the ark of the covenant and the possibility that the God of the Israelites might be real

(and stronger than their own). In what ways do you hedge your bets with God? Why are we tempted to do this? What does it say about your faith?

13. Have you ever bargained with God in order to get some kind of guarantee from Him? Explain. What led you to attempt this approach to God? How did the circumstance play out?

Going Forward

14. Think of one or two things that you have learned that you'd like to work on in the coming week. Remember that this is all about quality, not quantity. It's better to work on one specific area of life and do it well than to work on many and do poorly (or to be so overwhelmed that you simply don't try).

Do you need to identify and give up false idols? Be specific. Go back through 1 Samuel 4—11 and put a star next to the phrase or verse that is most encouraging to you. Consider memorizing this verse.

Real-Life Application Ideas: Take some time this week to identify the idols in your life. Be tough on yourself here—some things you count on may appear to be good, but if they take your eyes off of God, they're probably idols. As you consider the things that distract you from God, look for practical ways to change your approach to them. For example, if sports have become an idol to you, perhaps you need to cut back on watching TV or participating in activities. Avoid overthinking this, though. Ask for wisdom from family and friends, and be sure to ask God for guidance as well.

Seeking Help

15. Write a prayer below (or simply pray one in silence), inviting God to work on your mind and heart in those areas you've noted in the Going Forward section. Be honest about your desires and fears.

Notes for Small Groups:

- *Look for ways to put into practice the things you wrote in the Going Forward section. Talk with other group members about your ideas and commit to being accountable to one another.*

- *During the coming week, ask the Holy Spirit to continue to reveal truth to you from what you've read and studied.*

- *Before you start the next lesson, read 1 Samuel 12— 15. For more in-depth lesson preparation, read chapters 4, "Reviewing and Rebuking," and 5, "A Foolish Vow and a Lame Excuse" in* Be Successful.

Rebukes and Excuses

(1 SAMUEL 12—15)

Before you begin ...

- *Pray for the Holy Spirit to reveal truth and wisdom as you go through this lesson.*
- *Read 1 Samuel 12—15. This lesson references chapters 4 and 5 in* Be Successful. *It will be helpful for you to have your Bible and a copy of the commentary available as you work through this lesson.*

Getting Started

From the Commentary

Saul and the people rejoiced greatly over the deliverance of Jabesh Gilead from the Ammonites, and Saul was careful to give the glory to the Lord (1 Sam. 11:13). Samuel saw the victory as a great opportunity to "renew the kingdom" (v. 14) and remind the people that Jehovah God was still their King. The fact that Saul had led the army in a great victory would tempt the Israelites to put their faith in their new king, and Samuel wanted them to know that their future success rested in trusting Jehovah alone. The king was only God's servant for the people, and both king and people had to obey God's covenant. In his farewell message, Samuel defended his own ministry (12:1–5), reviewed God's mercies to Israel (vv. 6–11), and admonished the people to fear the Lord and obey the covenant (vv. 12–25).

—*Be Successful*, page 69

1. Samuel mentions the Lord at least thirty times in his farwell message. Why? What are the risks of giving credit to man instead of God? What are examples of this in today's church?

2. Choose one verse or phrase from 1 Samuel 12—15 that stands out to you. This could be something you're intrigued by, something that makes you uncomfortable, something that puzzles you, something that resonates with you, or just something you want to examine further. Write that here.

Going Deeper

From the Commentary

In asking for a king, the people had rejected the kingship of Jehovah and the leadership of Samuel, the last of the judges (7:6, 15–17). It must have been painful for Samuel to conduct this last meeting as their leader and transfer the civil authority to Saul. No doubt he had hoped that one of his sons would succeed him, but they weren't even considered (8:1–3). The twelve tribes had been governed by judges for nearly 500 years, but times had changed and the people wanted a king. Before leaving office as judge, Samuel had to set the record straight and bear witness that his hands were clean and the people could find no fault in him.

To many of the people at that assembly, Samuel had "always been there." Some of them had known him when he was a child and youth at Shiloh, learning to serve as a priest, and others remembered when he had begun to proclaim the Word of the Lord (3:20). He had walked before them almost all of his life, and now he stood before them "old and gray-headed" and challenged them to accuse him of using his authority to benefit himself. "Here I am" (12:3) makes us think of Samuel's responses the night the Lord called him (3:4–6, 8, 16). In the East, it was expected that civil officials would use their offices to make money, but Samuel hadn't taken that route. He obeyed the law of Moses and kept his hands clean (Ex. 20:17; 22:1–4, 9; 23:8; Lev. 19:13; Deut. 16:19; 24:14).

With such a godly example before them, we wonder why his sons took bribes.

—*Be Successful*, pages 69–70

3. Review 1 Samuel 12:1–5. Why was it important that Samuel present himself as a man of integrity? How did he do this? Why was it important that Samuel get the people's vote of confidence about the king?

From the Commentary

Having affirmed Samuel's credibility, the people now had to accept his analysis of the situation. He reviewed Israel's history from Moses to his own day and emphasized what the Lord in His grace had done for them.

It was God, not the people, who appointed Moses and Aaron (v. 6) and who enabled them to do the mighty works they did for the people of Israel. Samuel wasn't afraid to point out Israel's sins and then challenge them to devote themselves to the Lord and to His covenant. It's often been said that the one thing we learn from history is

that we don't learn from history, and Samuel didn't want
his people to make that mistake.

—*Be Successful*, page 71

4. Review 1 Samuel 12:6–11. In what ways was this like a court trial? What
was Samuel trying to prove? Why? What was the covenant God had made
with the people? How is this significant in Samuel's speech?

*More to Consider: Samuel "prayed up a storm" during the dry season
of wheat harvest (mid-May to mid-June). What was the purpose of
this miracle? Read Exodus 8:8; 9:27–28; and 10:16–17. How was
the Israelites' response to Samuel's act similar to Pharaoh's response to
Moses? How was this storm a demonstration of God's power? How did
it put the king in his place?*

From the Commentary

The narrative in chapters 13—15 focuses on Saul's early
reign, especially his relationship to God and to Samuel.

We see Saul making foolish and unwise decisions and trying to cover his disobedience with lies. It was the beginning of that tragic decline that ended in a witch's house and Saul's suicide on the battlefield. At chapter 16, David will come on the scene, and the book will describe Saul's deepening conflict with God, himself, and David. We can trace the downward steps in Saul's tragic failure.

—*Be Successful*, page 74

5. Review 1 Samuel 13:1–14. How did each of the following contribute to Saul's decline: pride (see vv. 1–4); unbelief and impatience (see vv. 5–9); deception (see vv. 10–12); folly (see vv. 13–14)? How do these same issues trip up believers today?

From the Commentary

Saul had mustered over 300,000 men to rescue the people of Jabesh Gilead and then had cut it down to 3,000, but now his forces numbered only 600. The Philistine army was "as the sand which is on the seashore in multitude" (v. 5), a simile also used for the army Gideon faced (Judg.

7:12)—and Saul's army was twice as large as Gideon's! The difference wasn't so much the size of the army as the strength of the leader's faith. Gideon trusted God for victory and God honored him; Saul disobeyed God and God punished him. Saul had mustered that huge army by means of fear (1 Sam. 11:7), so when his men began to fear the enemy instead of the king, they began to desert the camp and go to places of safety.

—*Be Successful*, page 78

6. What does 1 Samuel 13:15–23 reveal about the condition of the army of Israel under Saul's leadership? In what ways did Saul walk by sight rather than by faith? How does this compare and contrast to Jonathan's leadership (see chapter 14)?

From the Commentary

The focus in chapter 14 is on Jonathan, Saul's oldest son, who had won the first major battle against the Philistines, but his father had taken the credit (13:1–7). It's a remarkable blessing of the grace of God that a man like Saul should have a son so magnificent as Jonathan. He was a courageous warrior (2 Sam. 1:22), a born leader, and a man of faith who sought to do the will of God. As the account progresses, it becomes clear that Saul is jealous of Jonathan and his popularity, and this jealousy increases when Jonathan and David become devoted friends.

The Philistines had sent a detachment of soldiers to establish a new outpost to guard the pass at Michmash (1 Sam. 13:23), and Jonathan saw this as an opportunity to attack and see the Lord work. Saul was hesitating in unbelief (14:2) while his son was acting by faith. God had called Saul to begin Israel's liberation from the Philistines, but most of the time he only followed up on what others started. In spite of all that the Lord had done for him and all that Samuel had taught him, Saul was not a man of faith who trusted the Lord and sought to glorify Him. Saul had a priest of the Lord attending him, a man named Ahiah from the rejected line of Eli (v. 3), but the king never waited for the Lord's counsel (vv. 18–20). Saul is a tragic example of the popular man of the world who tries to appear religious and do God's work, but who lacks a living faith in God and a heart to honor Him. Unfortunately, church history records the lives of too many gifted people who "used God" to achieve their own purposes, but in the end abandoned Him and ended life in disgrace.

—Be Successful, pages 83–84

7. Why didn't Jonathan tell his father that he had a plan to rout the enemy? What makes Jonathan's faith so admirable in this situation?

From the Commentary

The spiritual conditions of our hearts are revealed not only by the actions we perform but also by the words we speak. "For out of the abundance of the heart the mouth speaketh" (Matt. 12:34). When you read King Saul's words recorded in Scripture, they often reveal a heart controlled by pride, foolishness, and deceit. He would say foolish things just to impress people with his "spirituality," when in reality he was walking far from the Lord.

Saul's heart was not right with God and he foolishly forced his army to agree to a vow of fasting until evening (1 Sam. 14:24). He didn't impose this fast because it was the will of God but because he wanted his soldiers to think he was a man wholly dedicated to the Lord. But this command was only more evidence of Saul's confused and superstitious faith. He thought that their fasting plus the presence of the ark would impress the Lord and He would give them victory. But Jonathan and his armor-bearer were already enjoying victory without either the ark or the fast!

No sensible commander would deprive his troops of food and energy while they were fighting the enemy. If the Lord commands it, then He would give the strength needed, but God gave Saul no such commission. Moses had fasted for forty days and nights when he was on the mountain with the Lord (Ex. 34:28), for the Lord sustained him. But Saul's soldiers were "distressed" (1 Sam. 14:24), "faint" (v. 28), and "very faint" (v. 31) because of this unnecessary fast. When we obey God's commands, we walk by faith, but when we obey unnatural human regulations, we only tempt the Lord. The first is confidence but the second is presumption. All of us need to heed the admonition given in Ecclesiastes 5:2—"Do not be rash with your mouth, and let not your heart utter anything hastily before God" (NKJV).

When Jonathan and his armor-bearer joined the Israelite army in their march, they knew nothing about the king's foolish command, and Jonathan ate some honey from a honeycomb that had dropped to the ground. Then one of the soldiers told him that his father had put a curse on any soldier who ate any food that day. Why hadn't somebody warned Jonathan sooner? Perhaps they hoped that his innocent "disobedience" would open the way for all of them to eat! We wonder if Saul wasn't deliberately putting his son's life in jeopardy. However, Jonathan wasn't too worried, and he even dared to admit that his father's leadership had brought trouble to the land (1 Sam. 14:29).

—*Be Successful,* pages 87–88

8. Review 1 Samuel 14:24–52. Is it surprising the lengths King Saul went to in order to present himself as a godly man? Why or why not? How is this sort of pretending an issue even in today's church? What is so appealing about the appearance of godliness that makes believers lie in order to convince others of it?

More to Consider: When Jews slaughtered their animals, they were required to drain out the blood before preparing the meat, for blood was never to be used as food (Lev. 3:17; 7:26; 17:10–14; Deut. 12:23–24; see Gen. 9:4). In what ways did Saul's carnal vow bring out the worst in people? Why was his attempt to turn a gastronomical orgy into a worship service doomed to failure? What lessons can we draw from this mistake to help avoid similar moral failures in the church today?

From the Commentary

> Chapter 15 is a pivotal chapter in the story of Saul. The Lord gave him another opportunity to prove himself, but he failed again, lied about it, and was judged. Saul had a habit of substituting saying for doing and of making excuses instead of confessing his sins. No matter what happened, it was always somebody else's fault. He was more concerned about looking good before the people than being good before God.
>
> —*Be Successful*, page 91

9. How did Saul fail in chapter 15? What would success have looked like in God's eyes? What does this continued failure say about Saul's character? Why did God let him continue in a leadership position if he was so ungodly?

From the Commentary

> Saul had once been a modest young man (9:21), but now for the second time he had willfully disobeyed the Lord's will and even erected a monument in honor of the event.

He was to annihilate a nation that for centuries had done evil, but he ended up doing evil himself. Confronted with this accusation, Saul began to argue with God's servant and deny that he had done wrong. For the second time he lied when he said, "I have obeyed" (15:13, 20); for the second time he blamed his army (vv. 15, 21); and for the second time he used the feeble excuse of dedicating the spared animals as sacrifices for the Lord (vv. 15, 21).

The prophet rejected all three lies and explained why God couldn't accept the animals as legitimate sacrifices: The Lord wants living obedience from the heart, not dead animals on the altar. God doesn't need any donations from us (Ps. 50:7–15), and the sacrifice He desires is a broken and contrite heart (51:16–17). Sacrifice without obedience is only hypocrisy and empty religious ritual (Isa. 1:11–17; Jer. 7:21–26; Ps. 40:6–8). "For I desired mercy, and not sacrifice; and the knowledge of God more than burnt offerings" (Hos. 6:6). The religious leaders in Jesus' day didn't understand this truth (Matt. 9:9–13; 12:1–8), although occasionally somebody in the crowd would see the light (Mark 12:28–34).

Samuel was a Levite and a prophet, so he certainly wasn't criticizing the Jewish sacrificial system. The Lord through Moses had established Jewish worship, and it was right for the people to bring their sacrifices to the Lord. This was His appointed way of worship. But the worshippers had to come to the Lord with submissive hearts and genuine faith, or their sacrifices were in vain. When David was in the wilderness and away from the priests and the sanctuary of God, he knew that God would accept worship from his heart. "Let my prayer be set before you as incense, the lifting up of my hands as the evening sacrifice" (Ps. 141:2 NKJV). Christian worship today must be more than simply going through a liturgy; we must worship God "in spirit and in truth" (John 4:24), "singing with grace in your hearts to the Lord" (Col. 3:16 NKJV).

—*Be Successful*, pages 93–94

10. What evidence do we have that the sins of rebellion and stubbornness controlled Saul's heart? How are these sins a form of idolatry?

Looking Inward

Take a moment to reflect on all that you've explored thus far in this study of 1 Samuel 12—15. Review your notes and answers and think about how each of these things matters in your life today.

Tips for Small Groups: To get the most out of this section, form pairs or trios and have group members take turns answering these questions. Be honest and as open as you can in this discussion, but most of all, be encouraging and supportive of others. Be sensitive to those who are going through particularly difficult times and don't press for people to speak if they're uncomfortable doing so.

11. Are you more like Samuel or Saul when it comes to obeying God? Explain. When you're acting more like Samuel, how does that affect your inner spirit? Your relationship with God? Your practical faith life? How about when you're acting more like Saul?

12. Have you ever "puffed yourself up" or put on a false face to impress others with your piety or apparent godliness? What prompted that action? Is it important for you to be perceived as godly? Why or why not? What does God think about such things?

13. Think of a time you made an excuse for a behavior that wasn't godly, or for not doing something that God was leading you to do. What did you think to accomplish by presenting God with an excuse? Why is it so tempting to explain away errors of judgment rather than own up to them? How can owning up to our mistakes help us grow closer to God?

Going Forward

14. Think of one or two things that you have learned that you'd like to work on in the coming week. Remember that this is all about quality, not quantity. It's better to work on one specific area of life and do it well than to work on many and do poorly (or to be so overwhelmed that you simply don't try).

Do you want to examine your life for times when you are focused on appearing godly? Be specific. Go back through 1 Samuel 12—15 and put a star next to the phrase or verse that is most encouraging to you. Consider memorizing this verse.

Real-Life Application Ideas: These chapters in 1 Samuel present two distinctly different approaches to following God. Samuel shows us a man of integrity and Saul shows us a man who is a great pretender. Sit down with a trusted friend this week to talk about your own spiritual integrity. Use the time to honestly assess your character and how you live out (or fail to live out) a godly character in the everyday ebb and flow of life. If you discover areas of weakness, talk together about practical ways you can address those through prayer, counsel, and teaching.

Seeking Help

15. Write a prayer below (or simply pray one in silence), inviting God to work on your mind and heart in those areas you've noted in the Going Forward section. Be honest about your desires and fears.

Notes for Small Groups:

- *Look for ways to put into practice the things you wrote in the Going Forward section. Talk with other group members about your ideas and commit to being accountable to one another.*

- *During the coming week, ask the Holy Spirit to continue to reveal truth to you from what you've read and studied.*

- *Before you start the next lesson, read 1 Samuel 16—17. For more in-depth lesson preparation, read chapter 6, "God Chooses a King" in* Be Successful.

A Chosen King
(1 SAMUEL 16—17)

Before you begin ...
- *Pray for the Holy Spirit to reveal truth and wisdom as you go through this lesson.*
- *Read 1 Samuel 16—17. This lesson references chapter 6 in* Be Successful. *It will be helpful for you to have your Bible and a copy of the commentary available as you work through this lesson.*

Getting Started

From the Commentary

Anyone who has ever been deeply disappointed by a friend or family member can understand why aged Samuel mourned so long over King Saul. Israel had rejected Samuel's leadership over them because he was too old, and they didn't want his sons to succeed him because they accepted bribes and perverted justice (1 Sam. 8:3). But King Saul was guilty of disobeying God's clear commandments and also of lying about what he had done, and because of these sins, he had forfeited his throne. He was still in office and yet was unfit to lead the nation, and Samuel had broken fellowship with him (15:34–35).

—*Be Successful*, page 99

1. How must Samuel have felt as he watched Saul fail miserably as a king? How is this similar to the way search committee members feel when they choose a pastor who doesn't live up to their hopes and expectations? What is a follower's responsibility to his or her leaders? How can we help hold our leaders accountable?

More to Consider: The word translated "mourn" means "to mourn for the dead." How is this an accurate description of Samuel's sorrow? There is a time to mourn (Eccl. 3:4), but there is also a time to act (Josh. 7:10). How had that time arrived for Samuel? Was Samuel's work over yet? What does this reveal about our timing versus God's timing?

2. Choose one verse or phrase from 1 Samuel 16—17 that stands out to you. This could be something you're intrigued by, something that makes

you uncomfortable, something that puzzles you, something that resonates with you, or just something you want to examine further. Write that here.

Going Deeper

From the Commentary

> Had an election been held in Israel to choose a replacement for King Saul, it's not likely that the people would have chosen David, but he was God's first choice. "He also chose David his servant, and took him from the sheepfolds; from following the ewes that had young he brought him, to shepherd Jacob his people, and Israel his inheritance" (Ps. 78:70–71 NKJV). Let's consider some facts about this unusual young man.
>
> In spite of the fact that it was a small town in Judah, Bethlehem was a well-known place to the Jewish people. It was when Jacob and his family were on their way to Bethel that his favorite wife, Rachel, died near Bethlehem while giving birth to Benjamin (Gen. 35:16–20). It was in Bethlehem that Ruth, the widow from Moab, found her husband, Boaz, and gave birth to Obed, David's grandfather (Ruth 4:13–22; Matt. 1:3–6). David himself would

make Bethlehem a famous place, and so would Jesus, the
son of David, who would be born there as the Scriptures
promised (Mic. 5:2; Matt. 2:6).

—*Be Successful*, page 100

3. Bethlehem means "house of bread." How does this add resonance to
God's choice of David as the next king? Why did God choose a king from
such a small town and from such an unusual occupation? What message
does this have for us in the church today, regarding our leaders?

From the Commentary

Before the guests sat down to enjoy the fellowship feast,
Samuel looked over seven of Jesse's sons, thinking that
the whole family was there, but he was operating by sight
and not by faith. We don't know what Samuel's two sons
looked like, but we do know that their father admired
men who were handsome and well-built. Samuel had
already forgotten this mistake he had made about Saul
(1 Sam. 9:2; 10:23–24). David was the eighth son and
only six of his brothers are named in Scripture: Eliab,

the firstborn; Abinadab, the second; Shimea, the third, also called Shammah; Nethanel, or Nathaniel, the fourth; Raddai, the fifth; and Ozem, the sixth (1 Chron. 2:13–15). David is called the seventh in this genealogy, but 1 Samuel 16:10–11 makes it clear that he was the eighth and youngest son. Apparently one brother died without issue, and his name dropped out of the genealogy. David also had two sisters: Zeruiah was the mother of Abishai, Joab, and Asahel; and Abigail, who was the mother of Amasa (1 Chron. 2:16–17). All of these men played important roles in David's kingdom.

—*Be Successful*, page 101

4. Review 1 Samuel 16:6–10. Why was David's family the perfect family from which to choose a new leader? With so many capable men, why would God choose the one who seemed least capable? (See 1 Chron. 28:9; Jer. 17:10; Rom. 8:27; Heb. 4:12.) How does God's choice of David give all believers today hope that they can be used by God in surprising ways?

From Today's World

Politics and religion are two of the hottest hot-button topics that exist in society today (and have been for centuries). And when it comes to choosing our leaders (whether in government or churches), there are no limits to the lengths people will go to support or impugn a given candidate. In the modern age, our access to information makes it easier than ever to learn about anyone being considered for leadership. And social media gives supporters and detractors alike bully pulpits to spread their opinions (often presented as fact, whether or not there is any truth in the content) far and wide.

5. Is it easier or harder to choose leaders in the Internet age? Explain. What are the benefits of instant access to information? What are the challenges? Where does God sit in the midst of all our leadership decisions? How can we use the strengths of social media to bring God into the discussions rather than exclude Him? Why is it important to seek God's wisdom when it comes to choosing leaders in secular government?

From the Commentary

God's pattern for leadership is stated in Matthew 25:21—
"Well done, good and faithful servant; you were faithful
over a few things, I will make you ruler over many things.

Enter into the joy of your Lord" (NKJV). David had been faithful as a servant over a few things, and God promoted him to being a ruler over many things—from a flock to a whole nation! Unlike Saul, David could be trusted with exercising authority because he had been under authority and had proved himself faithful.

—*Be Successful*, pages 102–103

6. Read about Moses (Ex. 3), Gideon (Judg. 6), Elisha (1 Kings 19:19–21), Nehemiah (Neh. 1), Amos (Amos 7:14–15), Peter, Andrew, James, and John (Mark 1:16–20), and Matthew (Matt. 9:9–13). In what ways were all these men busy and engaged in life when God called them? What occupied David's life when God called him? What does that tell us about the kind of people God wants for leaders?

From the Commentary

While the physical appearance wasn't the most important thing for a king (1 Sam. 16:7), David was so striking in his appearance that the Lord calls our attention to it. Saul was different from most Semitic people of that day because he was tall, but David's distinctive was that he was fair rather than swarthy. The word translated "ruddy" is the same as Esau's nickname "Edom—red" (Gen. 25:24–34). Some have interpreted this to mean that David was a redhead, but it may only mean that, unlike the average Semite, he was fair of skin and hair. Like Joseph, he was handsome (39:6) and had a winsome personality (1 Sam. 16:18). He was the kind of person who attracted people and won and held their confidence.

—Be Successful, page 103

7. It seems that looks mattered in God's choice of David as king. But the kind of looks went against common wisdom of the time. Why would God choose someone the people wouldn't consider "kingly" to be a king? What role did David's personality play in his selection as king? How did it compare to Saul's? David gets into all kinds of trouble later in life. What does this say about God's original choice of him as king?

From the Commentary

David knew that the Lord had been present at his conception and had arranged for his genetic structure (Ps. 139:13–16). He ordained that David would be strong and handsome, that he would possess musical talent, that he would be prudent and brave. Just as Paul was a vessel prepared by God for a specific work (Gal. 1:15; Acts 9:15), so David was God's prepared servant to accomplish His purposes for His people.

Saul's attendants knew that something was seriously wrong with their master, and they rightly attributed it to the attacks of an evil spirit. God had permitted this spirit to trouble Saul (1 Sam. 16:14, 23; 18:10; 19:9) as part of His discipline because of the king's rebellion. By nature, Saul was a suspicious and revengeful man, and this gave the evil spirit a beachhead for his operations (Eph. 4:25–27). The one man in the kingdom who was prepared to minister to Saul was David!

David was a poet and musician, skilled at playing the harp and composing songs. By the end of his life, he was known as "the sweet psalmist of Israel" (2 Sam. 23:1). It's unusual to find such artistic talent in a man who was also a rugged soldier and fearless general. He wrote psalms, organized the music ministry for the temple (1 Chron. 25), and provided instruments for the musicians (23:5). From the spoils of his many battles, he provided the materials for the temple, and he longed to have the privilege of building a house for the Lord.

—*Be Successful*, pages 104–105

8. Review 1 Samuel 16:14–23. Why is it significant that David was a poet and musician? What does this reveal about God's character that previous leaders (the judges and Saul) did not? How did David's uniqueness qualify him for the role of a king? In what ways were the Israelites ready for a king like David? In what ways would God's choosing David have caused them concern?

More to Consider: Read 1 Samuel 16:18. In what ways does this verse reveal the key to David's success? (See 18:12, 14, 28.) Compare this to the success of other great biblical characters like Joseph (Gen. 39:2–3, 21, 23); Joshua (Josh. 6:27); and Samuel (1 Sam. 3:19). In what ways is this basis for success in the Christian life today? What does it mean for God to be "with" someone?

From the Commentary

David didn't remain in Saul's camp permanently but went back and forth between the camp and home as he was needed (1 Sam. 16:15 NIV). Whenever he was called to help Saul, he left his flock with a dependable man (v. 20) and hurried to the camp where now he even had his own tent (v. 54). It wasn't until after David killed Goliath that Saul took him permanently to be one of his armor-bearers (18:1–2). David was a Spirit-led man, and his every decision had to be in the will of God and for the glory of God. Others might come and go as they pleased, but David was guided by the providential hand of God. We can see the guidance of God in the events reported in chapter 17.

Goliath is described as standing nine feet, nine inches tall; wearing a coat of mail that weighed 125 pounds; and carrying a spear that weighed 15 pounds. He was a formidable opponent indeed. He had presented himself to the army of Israel each morning and evening for forty days, and apparently David arrived on the final day (17:16ff.). Jesse chose just the right day to send David to the battlefield to carry food supplies to his three brothers and their commanding officer (vv. 17–18). Unlike modern armies, soldiers in ancient armies had to provide their own rations and help provide for others.

David was up very early that day and heard the morning challenge that Goliath gave to Saul and his army. If the Israelites could provide a champion who was able to defeat Goliath, the Philistines would submit to the Jews and be their servants, but if not, the Israelites must consider themselves defeated and become the servants of the Philistines (vv. 8–9). Unfortunately, nobody in the Jewish army volunteered, including King Saul, who stood head and shoulders above his men. Since Israel had come to a crisis in this confrontation, Saul made a generous offer to the man who would silence Goliath: He would marry one of the king's daughters, receive great riches from the king, and take his father's house off the tax rolls. Saul hoped that somebody would be tempted by the offer and try to defeat Goliath.

—Be Successful, pages 106–107

9. What was David's response to Goliath's speech? Contrast this response to that offered by most of the Jewish army. What did God accomplish in using David to confront Goliath? What bigger message did He give His people?

From the Commentary

David had experienced the power of God in his own life, and he knew that the Lord could turn weakness into power. While caring for the sheep, David had killed a lion and a bear, and he knew that the Lord could deliver him out of the hand of Goliath. It's as though he sees Goliath as just another animal attacking God's flock! Saul knew nothing personally about this wonderful power of God, so he advised David to wear his armor. Saul didn't have the faith to believe that God could do something new, so he suggested the old-fashioned time-honored method of warfare. King Saul was a grown man and a large one at that, and David was only a teenager, so imagine what the armor looked like on David's body! But men and women of faith obey God no matter what the experts say.

—*Be Successful*, page 108

10. Where did David's encouragement come from? (See 1 Sam. 30:6.) What are some ways God rewarded David for trusting Him? How does God reward us today for trusting Him?

Looking Inward

Take a moment to reflect on all that you've explored thus far in this study of 1 Samuel 16—17. Review your notes and answers and think about how each of these things matters in your life today.

> *Tips for Small Groups: To get the most out of this section, form pairs or trios and have group members take turns answering these questions. Be honest and as open as you can in this discussion, but most of all, be encouraging and supportive of others. Be sensitive to those who are going through particularly difficult times and don't press for people to speak if they're uncomfortable doing so.*

11. David was an unlikely choice for king for a number of reasons. What are some of the things about you that make you wonder if you're a good representative for God? How can God use your inadequacies and self-doubt for His purposes? What are some ways God is already using you, despite what others might say about your qualifications?

12. What are some of the challenges you're facing right now? How are they like David's challenge when he faced Goliath? What are the weapons God

has given you to help face your challenge? What role does faith play in facing challenging circumstances?

13. What does trusting God look like to you in a practical sense? What does it mean to you to be "rewarded by God"? How do you know God is rewarding you? Is a reward from God anything like the worldly rewards we give one another? Explain.

Going Forward

14. Think of one or two things that you have learned that you'd like to work on in the coming week. Remember that this is all about quality, not quantity. It's better to work on one specific area of life and do it well than to work on many and do poorly (or to be so overwhelmed that you simply don't try).

Do you want to learn how you can better face the Goliaths in your life? Be specific. Go back through 1 Samuel 16—17 and put a star next to the phrase or verse that is most encouraging to you. Consider memorizing this verse.

Real-Life Application Ideas: With the guidance and counsel of your small group, identify a Goliath that your church is currently facing. This could be financial challenges, membership problems, community needs, or any other issue that seems too big to solve. Take an evening this week to brainstorm with your group members some practical ways to attack this problem. Be creative and don't presume the easy answer is the right one. Remember that God used a shepherd boy to defeat a giant. Be sure to spend plenty of time in prayer, asking God to show you the right "weapons" to use when battling this challenge.

Seeking Help

15. Write a prayer below (or simply pray one in silence), inviting God to work on your mind and heart in those areas you've noted in the Going Forward section. Be honest about your desires and fears.

Notes for Small Groups:

- *Look for ways to put into practice the things you wrote in the Going Forward section. Talk with other group members about your ideas and commit to being accountable to one another.*

- *During the coming week, ask the Holy Spirit to continue to reveal truth to you from what you've read and studied.*

- *Before you start the next lesson, read 1 Samuel 18— 19. For more in-depth lesson preparation, read chapter 7, "A Jealous King," in* Be Successful.

Jealousy
(1 SAMUEL 18—19)

Before you begin ...
- *Pray for the Holy Spirit to reveal truth and wisdom as you go through this lesson.*
- *Read 1 Samuel 18—19. This lesson references chapter 7 in* Be Successful. *It will be helpful for you to have your Bible and a copy of the commentary available as you work through this lesson.*

Getting Started

From the Commentary

Jewish men had to be at least twenty years old before they could go to war (Num. 1:3), but David was probably only eighteen when he was made a high-ranking officer in the Jewish army (1 Sam. 18:5). From the beginning of his new assignment, David found himself in a life-threatening conflict with King Saul. David didn't *create* problems for Saul; he *revealed* the deep-seated problems that were already there. David was an honest man of faith, but Saul was a deceitful, scheming man of the world. With great humility, David had accepted his appointment as Israel's next king, while Saul was almost paranoid as he tried to protect his throne. God had abandoned Saul but had given His Spirit's power to David, and David moved from victory to victory as he led Saul's troops.

—*Be Successful*, page 115

1. What important lessons might David have learned while serving under a king like Saul? How did David's success on the battlefield fuel Saul's anger and growing paranoia? Why is jealousy such a dangerous and damaging trait?

2. Choose one verse or phrase from 1 Samuel 18—19 that stands out to you. This could be something you're intrigued by, something that makes you uncomfortable, something that puzzles you, something that resonates with you, or just something you want to examine further. Write that here.

Going Deeper

From the Commentary

> At one time, Saul loved David (16:21), "liked him very much," (NIV), but the king's attitude changed into jealousy and then hatred. The Lord was with David (18:12, 14, 28), however, and Saul was not permitted to harm him. During the ten years or so that David was a fugitive, the Lord not only thwarted Saul's plans repeatedly, but He even used the king's hostility to mature David and make him into a man of courage and faith.
>
> —*Be Successful*, pages 115–116

3. Review 1 Samuel 18:1–12. In what ways was David being prepared for the throne during Saul's reign? How did Saul's hatred make David's character grow? What are some ways similar trials today help to forge strong leaders?

More to Consider: Too many Bible readers still view David and Jonathan as two frolicsome teenagers who liked each other because they had many common interests, but this picture is shallow and inaccurate. Jonathan had to be at least twenty years old to be in his father's army, and the fact that Jonathan was already commanding one-third of that army and had won two great victories (13:1–4; 14:1ff.) indicates that he was a seasoned soldier and not a callow adolescent. How might your view of these two friends be different if there were fifteen or more years' difference in their ages? Does that change the narrative? What new insights can we gain about the value of friendship if this was indeed the case?

From the Commentary

Saul wasn't pleased with his son's friendship with David. For one thing, Jonathan was Saul's best commander and was needed to make the king look good. Saul was also afraid that Jonathan would divulge court secrets to David, and when Saul discovered that David was already anointed to succeed him, this made matters worse. He saw David as an enemy, a threat to his own son's future, although Jonathan didn't view it that way.

—*Be Successful*, page 116

4. What are some of the ways Saul nurtured himself on pride, jealousy, and fear? How might that have directly affected his ability to lead? What prompts a leader to become paranoid? How can leaders avoid falling into that trap? What role does God play in helping leaders lead with confidence?

From Today's World

In the Internet age, it's no longer news when a young man or woman appears on the scene as the leader of an influential company. Facebook's leadership is the prime example of this. The more technology drives our culture's commerce, the more likely it is that leaders will be younger and younger, since they're the ones usually at the forefront of technology. The wisdom that comes with age is no longer a prerequisite for company leadership.

5. In what ways is a young CEO like David? What are some of the strengths of having a young leader in today's world? What do we lose by having younger leaders? How does this apply to churches and church organizations? Are the young leaders of today as capable as David was during his time? What are the differences between then and now? How has God's role in the lives of young leaders changed between then and now?

From the Commentary

"The crucible for silver and the furnace for gold, but man is tested by the praise he receives" (Prov. 27:21 NIV). Just as the crucible and furnace test the metal and prepare it for use, so praise tests and prepares people for what God has planned for them. How we respond to praise reveals what we're made of and whether or not we're ready to take on new responsibilities. If praise humbles us, then God can use us, but if praise puffs us up, we're not yet ready for a promotion.

In his attitudes, conduct, and service, David was a complete success, and Saul's servants and the Jewish people recognized this and praised him publicly. This popular acclaim started after David's stunning defeat of Goliath, when the army of Israel chased the Philistines for ten miles, defeated them, and took their spoils (1 Sam. 17:52ff.). As Saul and his men returned to camp, the women met the victors and praised both Saul and David. In true Hebrew fashion, their praise was exaggerated, but in one sense it was true. David's victory over Goliath made it possible for the whole army of Israel to conquer the Philistines, so each soldier's achievement was really a triumph for David.

—*Be Successful*, page 117

6. In what ways was praise an important part of David's life? How did that play out in his psalms? What are the dangers of being praised by man? How do we hold tight to humility if we receive effusive praise? What temptations do we face if others are praised and we are not?

From the Commentary

"It is a dangerous crisis when a proud heart meets with flattering lips," said John Flavel, seventeenth-century British Presbyterian clergyman and author. What the women sang didn't seem to affect David, but their song enraged Saul. Saul had already forfeited the kingdom (15:28), but he still asked, "What can he have more but the kingdom?" Saul's response to David's success was exactly opposite that of John the Baptist when he was told of the great success of Jesus: "He must increase, but I must decrease" (John 3:30).

Envy is a dangerous and insidious enemy, a cancer that slowly eats out our inner life and leads us to say and do terrible things. Proverbs 14:30 rightly calls it "the rotten-ness of the bones." Envy is the pain we feel within when somebody achieves or receives what we think belongs to us. Envy is the sin of successful people who can't stand to see others reach the heights they have reached and eventually replace them. By nature, we are proud and want to be recognized and applauded, and from childhood we have been taught to compete with others. Dr. Bob Cook often reminded us that everybody wears a sign that reads, "Please make me feel important." Much modern advertising thrives on envy as it cleverly contrasts the "haves" and the "have-nots" and urges the "have-nots" to buy the latest products and keep up with the "haves." Envious people max out their credit cards to buy things they don't need just to impress people who really don't care!

—*Be Successful*, pages 117–118

7. Why is envy such a dangerous trait? How does envy lead to anger? Why is this troublesome? (See Matt. 5:21–26.) Why did David remain faithful to his king even though the king tried to kill him? What lesson can we take from this?

From the Commentary

"Faith is living without scheming," but Saul was better at scheming than at trusting God. If Saul disobeyed God, he always had a ready excuse to get himself out of trouble, and if people challenged his leadership, he could figure out ways to eliminate them. Possessed by anger and envy, and determined to hold on to his crown, Saul decided that young David had to be killed.

Since David was an excellent soldier and a born leader, the logical thing was to give him assignments that would take him away from the camp where the enemy could kill him. Saul made David commander over 1,000 and sent him to fight the Philistines. If David was killed in battle, it was the enemy's fault, and if he lost a battle but lived, his popularity would wane. But the plan didn't work because David won all the battles! After all, the Lord was with him and the power of God was upon him. Instead of eliminating David or diminishing his popularity, Saul's scheme only made him a greater hero to the people, and this increased Saul's fear of David all the more.

—*Be Successful*, pages 118–119

8. Review 1 Samuel 18:13–16. How did Saul's scheme to kill David backfire? What does this tell us about schemes that go against God's will? What are some modern examples of schemes that backfired and instead revealed God's power or glory?

More to Consider: When David's reply was reported to Saul, the devious king saw in it a great opportunity to attack his enemies and get rid of David at the same time. Saul told his servants to tell David that all that the king required for a bride price was one hundred foreskins from the "uncircumcised Philistines" (1 Sam. 18:25). Saul was certain that at some point in this endeavor, David would meet his death. Once again, Saul was using one of his daughters to help destroy an innocent man, and in this instance, it was a man she truly loved.

Why is such a gruesome story included in the Bible? What does God teach us through Saul's ugly request and David's unqualified success at accomplishing that goal? What does Saul's request reveal about his heart? What does David's success reveal about his own heart?

From the Commentary

Saul's mind and heart were so possessed by hatred for David that he openly admitted to Jonathan and the court attendants that he intended to have his son-in-law killed. Saul was now through with behind-the-scenes plots and was out to destroy David in the quickest way possible, and he ordered Jonathan and the royal attendants to join him in his endeavor. The hope of Israel lay in the heart and ministry of David, and yet Saul wanted to kill him! David would conquer Israel's enemies and consolidate the kingdom. He would gather much of the wealth used to build the temple. He would write psalms for the Levites to sing in praising God, and he would even design the musical instruments they played. God's covenant with

David would keep the light shining in Jerusalem during the dark days of the nation's decline, and the fulfillment of that covenant would bring Jesus Christ the Messiah into the world. No wonder Satan was so determined to kill David!

—*Be Successful*, pages 120–121

9. Review 1 Samuel 19:1–17. If Saul knew that the hope of Israel lay with David, why did he continue to seek his death? How does Saul's life give evidence to the reality of evil? How is this whole story a perfect example of God's covenant with His people?

From the Commentary

David fled to Samuel in Ramah, a godly friend he knew he could depend on, and Samuel took him to the fellowship of the prophets where they could worship God and seek His face. The word *naioth* means "dwellings" and was probably a section in Ramah where the "school of the prophets" assembled. There Samuel and David could worship and pray and ask God for wisdom, and the prophets would pray with them. But Saul's spies were everywhere, and they reported to Saul where he could find David. The king sent three different groups of soldiers to capture David, but when they arrived at the place where the prophets had assembled, they were immediately possessed by the Spirit and began to praise and worship God! The Hebrew word translated "prophesy" can mean "to sing songs and praise God" as well as "to foretell events." Saul's soldiers didn't become prophets; they only uttered words inspired by the Spirit of God.

—*Be Successful*, page 123

10. What weapons did God use to protect David and Samuel? (See 2 Cor. 10:4.) How is the way the soldiers were "possessed by the spirit" when Saul sent them to capture David a glimpse of the Holy Spirit's power yet to come after Jesus' ascension?

Looking Inward

Take a moment to reflect on all that you've explored thus far in this study of 1 Samuel 18—19. Review your notes and answers and think about how each of these things matters in your life today.

Tips for Small Groups: To get the most out of this section, form pairs or trios and have group members take turns answering these questions. Be honest and as open as you can in this discussion, but most of all, be encouraging and supportive of others. Be sensitive to those who are going through particularly difficult times and don't press for people to speak if they're uncomfortable doing so.

11. David's character was shaped through trial by fire. What are some of the challenges you've faced that have helped to make your faith grow? Do you tend to welcome those difficult times or rebel against them? How can the counsel of wise friends (as Jonathan offered to David) help you through difficult times?

12. How do you deal with praise? Do you welcome it? Fear it? Pursue it? Are you embarrassed by it? What are healthy ways to accept praise? To give it to others? To deal with times when others are praised and you are not?

13. God protected David in many different ways as Saul tried to kill him. What are some ways you've felt God's protective power in your life? What are some of the ways Satan has attempted to destroy you or your faith? How can you count on the Holy Spirit's power in those circumstances?

Going Forward

14. Think of one or two things that you have learned that you'd like to work on in the coming week. Remember that this is all about quality, not quantity. It's better to work on one specific area of life and do it well than to work on many and do poorly (or to be so overwhelmed that you simply don't try).

Do you want to pay more attention to how you respond to praise or the lack of praise? Be specific. Go back through 1 Samuel 18—19 and put a star next to the phrase or verse that is most encouraging to you. Consider memorizing this verse.

Real-Life Application Ideas: David and Jonathan had a special friendship. This week, honor your best friendships in practical and significant ways. Offer to help a friend with a project. Give them your ear if they need to talk. Share your material goods and time with them. And bathe them in prayer. Keep in mind that this isn't about showing how good a friend you can be, it's simply about being that friend. Do all these things with great humility.

Seeking Help

15. Write a prayer below (or simply pray one in silence), inviting God to work on your mind and heart in those areas you've noted in the Going Forward section. Be honest about your desires and fears.

Notes for Small Groups:

- *Look for ways to put into practice the things you wrote in the Going Forward section. Talk with other group members about your ideas and commit to being accountable to one another.*

- *During the coming week, ask the Holy Spirit to continue to reveal truth to you from what you've read and studied.*

- *Before you start the next lesson, read 1 Samuel 20—22. For more in-depth lesson preparation, read chapter 8, "David in Exile," in* Be Successful.

Exile

(1 SAMUEL 20—22)

Before you begin ...
- *Pray for the Holy Spirit to reveal truth and wisdom as you go through this lesson.*
- *Read 1 Samuel 20—22. This lesson references chapter 8 in* Be Successful. *It will be helpful for you to have your Bible and a copy of the commentary available as you work through this lesson.*

Getting Started

From the Commentary

David has been criticized and called impulsive because he left Ramah and his friend Samuel and fled to Gibeah to confer with Jonathan. But David knew that Saul's ecstatic experience would soon end and would leave his heart unchanged. Saul had promised Jonathan that he wouldn't try to kill David (1 Sam. 19:6), but he had already broken

that promise four times (vv. 20–24), so the wisest course
for David was to get away from Saul and go into hiding.

—*Be Successful,* page 127

1. Why wouldn't waiting in Gibeah have been an exercise in faith? In what ways was hanging around only a way of tempting God?

2. Choose one verse or phrase from 1 Samuel 20—22 that stands out to you. This could be something you're intrigued by, something that makes you uncomfortable, something that puzzles you, something that resonates with you, or just something you want to examine further. Write that here.

Going Deeper

From the Commentary

In all literature, David and Jonathan stand out as examples of devoted friends. Jonathan had the more difficult situation because he wanted to be loyal to his father while at the same time being a friend to the next king of Israel. Conflict of loyalties, especially in the family, is one of the most painful difficulties we face in the life of faith (Matt. 10:34–39), but Christ calls for supreme devotion to Him and His will for our lives.

David met Jonathan somewhere near Gibeah and wasted no time confronting his beloved friend with the key question: "What have I done that is so evil that your father wants to kill me?" David hadn't disobeyed any royal commands, incited any rebellion against the throne, or broken God's law, yet Saul was bent on destroying him. David knew that Saul was an envious man who wanted to keep the throne for himself and hand it on to his descendants, but David had faith that the Lord would remove Saul from the scene in His good time and in His own way (1 Sam. 26:7–11). David dearly loved Jonathan and didn't want to hurt him by criticizing his father, but now it was a matter of life or death.

—*Be Successful*, pages 127–128

3. Review 1 Samuel 20:1–23. David was in an awkward position, not to mention at great risk, when he spoke with Jonathan about Saul's intent to

kill him. How did he approach that delicate conversation? How did the friendship between David and Jonathan inform the way they chose to deal with Saul's hatred of David?

More to Consider: Saul had thrown his spear at David at least two times (18:10–11; 19:9–10), and he had sent three groups of soldiers to capture him and finally went to Ramah himself to do the job (19:20–24). Why wasn't Jonathan yet convinced that his father was a disturbed man out to destroy God's anointed king? What does this say about the power of loyalty? About the kind of blindness people can sometimes have about their own relatives? How did God draw the line for Jonathan between loyalty to his father and loyalty to his friend? How can we best prepare ourselves so we can see that line in our own lives?

From the Commentary

Jonathan offered to help in any way his friend suggested, and David proposed a simple test of Saul's true feelings. It was customary for each Jewish family to hold a feast at the new moon (Num. 10:10; 28:11–15; Ps. 81:3), and Saul would expect David to attend. If Saul's son-in-law and leading military hero didn't attend the feast, it would be an insult to the king as well as the family, so David's absence would help reveal Saul's genuine attitude toward David. If Saul became angry, then David's assessment was correct, but if Saul excused David and didn't press the matter, then Jonathan was correct. The only problem with this scheme was that it required Jonathan to lie by saying that David had gone to Bethlehem to attend his own family's feast. David would be hiding in the field and waiting for Jonathan to tell him whether or not it was safe to come home.

—*Be Successful*, pages 128–129

4. How did Jonathan safely get the message to David (1 Sam. 20:1–11)? What lesson is there in this secrecy that we can apply to challenges we face in the church today? When is it okay to resort to secret tactics to accomplish good things? How does this apply to our culture as a whole?

From Today's World

The pressure that public figures feel is often immense. Not only do they usually have significant responsibilities to their constituents or their fans, they're constantly under scrutiny by those same people. And especially today, with the prevalence and proliferation of social media, there is little chance of escaping the public eye even if one desires to do so. So when someone is accused of wrongdoing, people are quickly forced to take sides, often before all the facts are on the table. (And we don't always know which are facts and which are fabrications.) In traditional politics, party loyalty matters. Constituents often choose to ally with their party even when the party is supporting a policy they may not agree with.

5. What are the positive aspects of loyalty when it comes to supporting our leaders? When does loyalty become a problem? How are our churches like (and unlike) our secular governments when it comes to loyalty and support? Where should a believer's loyalty ultimately land?

From the Commentary

From verse 11 to verse 23, David is silent while Jonathan reviews the covenant they had made with each other (18:1–4). Jonathan even took an oath and promised to give David the correct message on the third day of the feast, so he would know whether the king was friendly or angry. Jonathan went beyond the immediate crisis to deal with future events. He knew that David would one day become king, and he prayed that the Lord would bless his reign. In their covenant, they agreed that Jonathan would serve next to David as second in command (23:16–18), and now Jonathan asked that if anything happened to him, David would promise not to wipe out his household, and David agreed. The phrase "the kindness of the Lord" (20:14) shows up in 2 Samuel 9 where David's compassionate care of Jonathan's crippled son, Mephibosheth, is described.

—*Be Successful*, page 129

6. Why did Jonathan reaffirm his oath to David? Why did he include the whole house of David (1 Sam. 20:16)? Why did he ask David to repeat the oath? How is their agreement like or unlike a "gentleman's agreement" in modern society? Are agreements based solely on trust common today? Why or why not? What role did God play in a covenant agreement like David and Jonathan had?

From the Commentary

On the first day of the feast, David hid himself by the stone of Ezel and waited for Jonathan's signal, for it was remotely possible that the king might be favorably inclined and welcome him back into the official circle.

Constantly afraid of personal attack, Saul sat with his back to the wall, his commander Abner next to him, and Jonathan across from his father. David's place next to Jonathan was empty, but the king said nothing about it, convinced that David was ceremonially unclean and therefore unable to eat a holy feast that day. The feast consisted primarily of meat from the new moon fellowship offerings, and anyone ceremonially unclean was prohibited from participating (Lev. 7:20–21). Perhaps David had touched something unclean, or he may have had intercourse with his wife (15:16–18). If so, all he had to do was separate himself from other people for that day, bathe his body, and change clothes, and he could come back into society the next day.

But when the men met for their meal the second day, again David was missing, which suggested to Saul that his son-in-law's absence was caused by something more serious than simple ritual defilement. An unclean person could remove the defilement in a day, but David had been missing for two days. Suspicious of anything out of the ordinary in his official staff, Saul asked Jonathan why David was absent, disdainfully calling him "the son of Jesse" rather than by his given name that was now so famous. Later, Saul would try to humiliate the high priest, Ahimelech, by calling him "the son of Ahitub" (1 Sam. 22:11–12).

—*Be Successful*, pages 130–131

7. Review 1 Samuel 20:24–42. How did the conversations between Jonathan and his father go? What happened after Jonathan slipped his lie into the conversation? Why did things start to go wrong?

From the Commentary

When hateful feelings are in the heart, it doesn't take much for angry words to come out of the mouth (Matt. 12:34–35). Saul had probably been brooding over how David had insulted him by refusing to attend the feast, and the longer he brooded, the more the fire raged within. But instead of attacking David, King Saul attacked his own son! Had the Lord not intervened back in Ramah, Saul would have killed David in the very presence of the prophet Samuel (1 Sam. 19:22–24), and now he reviled his own son while eating a holy feast!

The king's tirade seems to disparage his own wife, but rightly understood, his words describe his son as the lowest of the low. According to Saul, Jonathan's treachery in befriending David indicated that he was not Saul's son at all but the son of some other man, for a son of Saul would never betray his father. Therefore, Jonathan was slandering his own mother and saying she was a common prostitute, a rebel against the law of Moses, and a woman who practiced perversion. Because Jonathan helped David and didn't protect his father's throne, he had shamed his mother as much as if he had exposed her nakedness. She bore him to be the successor to his father, and now Jonathan had refused the crown in favor of the son of Jesse. The king was shouting, "You are no son of mine! You must be illegitimate!"

—*Be Successful*, pages 131–132

8. What was Saul's overriding reason for wanting David (and even Jonathan) dead? What threat did they pose to him or his reign? If God had already essentially taken the crown from Saul, why did Saul continue to pursue David? What role did pride play in Saul's story?

More to Consider: The meeting between David and Jonathan in 23:16–18 wasn't their last, but it was certainly a profoundly emotional farewell. They both wept, but David wept the most. He didn't know how many years of exile lay before him, and he might perhaps never see his beloved friend again. Read Genesis 31:55 and Acts 20:37. What do these passages and David and Jonathan's relationship reveal about Eastern people's comfort in sharing their emotions? Why do Westerners often try to hide their feelings? How can David and Jonathan's relationship serve as a model for how we express our love for one another today?

From the Commentary

When David fled to Nob, it marked the beginning of an exile that lasted about ten years (21:1—29:11). Not all of David's wilderness experiences are recorded, but enough history has been given to show us that he was a man of faith and courage. While it's difficult to determine the background of every psalm, it's likely that David's fugitive years are reflected in Psalms 7, 11—13, 16—17, 22, 25, 31, 34—35, 52—54, 56—59, 63—64, 142—143.

—*Be Successful*, page 133

9. Read Psalm 18. How is this psalm representative of David's songs of praise during his period of suffering? What message does David's season of suffering (and his response to it as recorded throughout Psalms) teach us about finding courage? Read these two passages that Jesus quoted: Psalms 22:1 and 31:5. What does this reveal to us about Jesus' love for David?

From the Commentary

King Saul, spear in hand (1 Sam. 18:10; 19:9; 26:7–22), was holding court under a tree on a hill near Gibeah when word came to him that his spies had discovered David's latest hiding place. This was probably the wilderness stronghold near the Dead Sea (1 Sam. 22:4–5), which explains why God sent the message to Gad that the company should return to Judah. Saul used this event as an occasion to berate his officers, all of whom were from his own tribe of Benjamin. Always suspicious of treachery in the official ranks, Saul reminded the men that he was king and therefore was the only one who could reward them for their faithful service. David attracted men who were willing to risk their lives for him, but Saul had to use bribery and fear to keep his forces together. Saul was sure that his officers were conspiring against him because they had refused to tell him that David and Jonathan had covenanted together concerning the kingdom. Jonathan was the leader of a conspiracy that included some of the very men Saul was addressing. These traitors were working for David because David had promised to reward them. Furthermore, Saul was sure that David was plotting to kill him!

—*Be Successful*, page 138

10. Why do bad leaders often resort to bribery and coercion with their followers? How do they use fear to motivate? Is this an effective leadership model? Why or why not? What does it say about a leader if his followers

follow willingly, even unto death? How is the loyalty David gained from his followers similar to the loyalty Jesus gained from His followers?

Looking Inward

Take a moment to reflect on all that you've explored thus far in this study of 1 Samuel 20—22. Review your notes and answers and think about how each of these things matters in your life today.

Tips for Small Groups: To get the most out of this section, form pairs or trios and have group members take turns answering these questions. Be honest and as open as you can in this discussion, but most of all, be encouraging and supportive of others. Be sensitive to those who are going through particularly difficult times and don't press for people to speak if they're uncomfortable doing so.

11. Have you ever had a misplaced loyalty or been blindly loyal to someone you shouldn't have? What led to your support for this person? Why was it a bad idea? What are some things you could have done to prevent making such a mistake?

12. Have you ever made a covenant with someone and sealed it only with a handshake? What was the purpose of the covenant? Why did you choose to trust each other rather than put the agreement on paper? What role did God play in your covenant?

13. What are some ways you've suffered from stubbornness or pride when dealing with others? Why is pride such an easy trap to fall into? What is the antidote to pride? How can you be intentional in avoiding the temptations of pride?

Going Forward

14. Think of one or two things that you have learned that you'd like to work on in the coming week. Remember that this is all about quality, not quantity. It's better to work on one specific area of life and do it well than to work on many and do poorly (or to be so overwhelmed that you simply don't try).

Do you want to address stubbornness or misplaced loyalty? Be specific. Go back through 1 Samuel 20—22 and put a star next to the phrase or verse that is most encouraging to you. Consider memorizing this verse.

Real-Life Application Ideas: Think about a situation where you're suffering from disappointment. Now write a psalm expressing your love for God in the midst of this disappointment. Be sincere about your frustrations with God, but celebrate His greater wisdom and thank Him for using this circumstance for His glory. Read your psalm aloud every day this week, trusting in God's ability to turn all your trials into triumphs.

Seeking Help

15. Write a prayer below (or simply pray one in silence), inviting God to work on your mind and heart in those areas you've noted in the Going Forward section. Be honest about your desires and fears.

Notes for Small Groups:

- *Look for ways to put into practice the things you wrote in the Going Forward section. Talk with other group members about your ideas and commit to being accountable to one another.*

- *During the coming week, ask the Holy Spirit to continue to reveal truth to you from what you've read and studied.*

- *Before you start the next lesson, read 1 Samuel 23—26. For more in-depth lesson preparation, read chapters 9, "David the Deliverer," and 10, "A Wise Woman and a Foolish King," in* Be Successful.

Wisdom and Foolishness
(1 SAMUEL 23—26)

Before you begin ...
- *Pray for the Holy Spirit to reveal truth and wisdom as you go through this lesson.*
- *Read 1 Samuel 23—26. This lesson references chapters 9 and 10 in* Be Successful. *It will be helpful for you to have your Bible and a copy of the commentary available as you work through this lesson.*

Getting Started

From the Commentary

In the second chapter of his book *Up from Slavery,* Booker T. Washington wrote, "I have learned that success is to be measured not so much by the position that one has reached in life as by the obstacles which he has overcome while trying to succeed." Measured by this standard—and it's a valid one—David was a very successful man. For ten years he was considered an outlaw, yet he fought the Lord's battles and delivered Israel from her enemies.

He lived with his faithful men in the forsaken places of the land and often had to flee for his life, yet he knew that the Lord would finally deliver him and give him the promised throne.

—*Be Successful,* page 145

1. Why was David's coronation as king so important to the Israelites? Why is it so important to all believers across the ages?

2. Choose one verse or phrase from 1 Samuel 23—26 that stands out to you. This could be something you're intrigued by, something that makes you uncomfortable, something that puzzles you, something that resonates with you, or just something you want to examine further. Write that here.

Going Deeper

From the Commentary

The spies of both David and Saul were active in the land, and David's spies reported that the Philistines were attacking Keilah. David paused to determine the will of God, a practice every leader needs to imitate, for it's easy for our own personal interests to get in the way of God's will. How did David discover God's will when Abiathar the priest hadn't yet arrived in the camp (23:6)? The prophet Gad was with David (22:5), and it's likely that he prayed to the Lord for direction. Once Abiathar arrived with the ephod, David had him inquire of the Lord when there were important decisions to make (v. 9; 25:32; 26:11, 23).

Once David got the go-ahead signal from the Lord, he mobilized his men, but they weren't too enthusiastic about his plans. It was acceptable to fight the Philistines, Israel's long-time enemies, but they didn't want to fight their own Jewish brothers. What if Saul turned against David and his men? The band of 600 men would then be caught between two armies! Unwilling to impose his own ideas on his men, David sought the Lord's will a second time, and once again he was told to go rescue the people of Keilah. It wasn't David's unbelief that created the problem, because he had faith in the Lord, but the fear in the hearts of his men made them unprepared for battle.

God more than kept His promise because He not only helped David slaughter the invading Philistines but also take a great amount of spoil from them. David moved into Keilah, which was a walled city, and it was there that Abiathar went when he fled from Nob carrying the precious ephod (22:20–23; 23:6). But Saul's spies were at work and learned that David was now in Keilah, a walled city with gates. Saul told his troops they were going to Keilah to rescue the city, but his real purpose was to capture David, and he was certain that David could not escape. Saul was not only willing to slaughter the priests of Nob, but he would have destroyed his own people in the city of Keilah just to lay hands on David.

—*Be Successful*, pages 146–147

3. Why was Saul willing to go to such great lengths to destroy David? What did he have to gain? What was driving Saul's behavior? What are some of the ways he'd lost perspective?

From the Commentary

While serving on Saul's staff, David had dodged the king's spears, thwarted an attempted kidnapping, and escaped the intended violence of three companies of soldiers and of Saul himself. Now that he was a fugitive with a price on his head and had over six hundred people to care for, David had to be very careful what he did and where he went. There might be another Doeg hiding in the shadows.

David's spies quickly let him know that Saul was planning to come to Keilah, so with Abiathar's help, David sought the Lord's guidance. His great concern was whether the people of Keilah would turn him and his men over to Saul. Since David had rescued the city from the Philistines, you would have expected the citizens to be grateful and to protect David, but such was not the case. The Lord warned David to get out of the city because the people were prepared to turn him over to the king. No doubt the people of Keilah were afraid that if they didn't cooperate with Saul, he would massacre them as he did the people in Nob. David recalled how pained he was because of the tragedy at Nob, and he didn't want another city wiped out because of him. He led his men out and they "kept moving from place to place" (v. 13 NIV) until they settled in the wilderness of Ziph (v. 14).

—*Be Successful*, page 147

4. Review 1 Samuel 23:7–29. How did the kingdom suffer when Saul put all his attention on finding and killing David? What lessons does this give leaders today about how to avoid losing focus or perspective? How do

Saul's actions also support the value of leaders having a good support team (and wise counsel)?

More to Consider: Ziph was a town fifteen miles southeast of Keilah in "the wilderness of Ziph," which was part of "the wilderness of Judah." This is a destitute area adjacent to the Dead Sea. Why did God lead David to this sort of area rather than a less desolate place? What sorts of temptations and trials would David have experienced in this place? How is this like and unlike Jesus' wilderness experience?

From the Commentary

Saul wasn't about to give up, so he followed David into the wilderness of Maon, and the two armies met at "the rock," a well-known mountain in the area. Saul divided his army and sent half around one side of the mountain and half around the other side, a pincer movement that would have meant total defeat for David and his 600 soldiers. But the Lord was in control and brought the Philistines to attack somewhere in Judah, and Saul and his men had to abandon the attack. It was a close call for David, but God kept His promises. To commemorate this great escape, the Jews called the place "Sela Hammahlekoth," which means "the rock of parting." The Hebrew carries the idea of "a smooth rock" and therefore "a slippery rock," in other words, "the rock of slipping away." David quickly moved from Maon to Engedi, next to the Dead Sea, a place of safety with an ample water supply.

—*Be Successful*, page 149

5. Read Psalm 54. What does this psalm (written around the time David went to Engedi) tell us about his state of mind? What does it reveal about his trust in God? How did David endure the constant barrage of lies being told about him?

From the Commentary

David and his men were hiding in a large cave, of which there were many in that area, and Saul chose to use that very cave as a place where he could relieve himself. The law of Moses was very strict when it came to matters of sanitation, especially in the army camp (Deut. 23:12–14). Each soldier was required to leave the camp to relieve himself, and he had to carry a small shovel or trowel among his weapons so he could dig a hole and cover his excrement. This meant that Saul was away from the camp and therefore quite vulnerable. He naturally wanted privacy and he felt that he was not in danger. The fact that he walked right into David's hiding place not only proved that his spies were incompetent but also that the Lord was still in control.

As David and his men pressed to the walls in the back of the cave, they quietly discussed the meaning of this remarkable occurrence. The men assured David that Saul's presence in the cave was the fulfillment of a promise God gave him that He would deliver Saul into David's hands. But when did God say this? Were they referring to Samuel's words to Saul in 1 Samuel 15:26–29, or to God's message to Samuel in 16:1? Perhaps the idea came from Jonathan's words in 20:15, which some of the men might have heard personally. It's likely that the leaders of the 600 men discussed these matters among themselves, for their future was wrapped up in David's future, and obviously they came to some false conclusions. David never planned to kill Saul, for he was sure that the Lord would remove him from the scene in His own way and His own time (26:9–11).

—Be Successful, page 150

6. Why was it tempting for David to kill Saul in this circumstance? Why didn't he take advantage of the opportunity? What does this say about David's relationship with God? About God's plans for Saul? For David?

From the Commentary

The death of Samuel, Israel's prophet and judge, is mentioned twice in the book (25:1; 28:3). Both references state that all Israel mourned his death and gathered to bury him. Of course, not every Israelite attended the funeral service, but the leaders of the tribes were present to pay their last respects to a great man. Since Saul and Samuel had been alienated for over seven years, it's not likely that the king attended the funeral, but he would call on Samuel for help even after the prophet was dead (chap. 28).

The people of Israel didn't always obey Samuel when he was alive, but they were careful to honor him when he died. Such is human nature (Matt. 23:29–31). However, Samuel didn't prepare an elaborate tomb for himself at some important public place, but instead asked to be buried at his own house in Ramah, probably in the garden or in a courtyard. In his pride, King Saul had prepared a public monument to himself at Carmel (1 Sam. 15:12), but Samuel, who truly deserved recognition, humbly asked to be laid to rest at his own home.

David knew it would be dangerous for him to attend the funeral at Ramah, for Saul would have his spies there, so he retreated to the wilderness. David had shown his love and respect for Samuel while the prophet was alive, so there was no need for him to make a public appearance.

—*Be Successful*, pages 157–158

7. How did Samuel's faith and courage help the nation transition from political disunity to a somewhat united monarchy? How had Samuel helped prepare David for his coming role as king? How is Samuel's life a model for seasoned leaders today?

From the Commentary

During David's previous stay in the wilderness of Maon (23:24ff.), which is in the vicinity of Carmel, his men had been a wall of protection for Nabal's flocks and those caring for them. Nabal was a very wealthy man, but he was not a generous man. When David returned to Nabal's neighborhood, it was shearing time, a festive event (2 Sam. 13:23) that occurred each spring and early fall. David hoped that Nabal would reward him and his men for their service, for certainly they deserved something for protecting Nabal's sheep and goats from the thieves that usually showed up at shearing time.

David's expectation was logical. Any man with 3,000 sheep and 1,000 goats could easily spare a few animals to feed 600 men who had risked their own lives to guard part of his wealth. Common courtesy would certainly dictate that Nabal invite David and his men to share his food at a festive season when hospitality was the order of the day. It wouldn't be easy to feed 600 men in the wilderness, so David sent ten of his young men to explain the situation and to ask to be invited to the feast. Nabal refused to listen.

—*Be Successful*, page 159

8. Review 1 Samuel 25:2–13. How is this story a good example of David's diplomacy? How does it illustrate his leadership abilities and his care and concern for his men? What lessons can today's leaders glean from this story?

More to Consider: The character of Nabal is described as "churlish and evil" (1 Sam. 25:3), which the NIV translates "surly and mean" in all his dealings. The man was like a stubborn, vicious animal that nobody could safely approach (1 Sam. 25:17). One of his own servants and his own wife both called him a son of Belial—a worthless fellow (vv. 17, 25). Read Deuteronomy 13:13; Judges 19:22; 20:13; and 1 Samuel 2:12. What do these passages tell us about a "wicked man"? What is the point of including the mention of Nabal's worthlessness? How does Nabal demonstrate the reality of evil in the world?

From the Commentary

Abigail was a woman of faith who believed that David was God's king, and she saw King Saul as only "a man" (1 Sam. 25:29). She quickly confessed that her husband was a "worthless fellow" (v. 25, see v. 17) who lived up to his name—fool—and she explained that she had known nothing about David's request for food. She accepted the blame for "this iniquity" (vv. 24, 28).

In the rest of her speech, Abigail focused on David and the Lord and not on David and Nabal, and her emphasis was on David's future. By now David was calming down and starting to realize that he was in the presence of a remarkable woman. She pointed out that the Lord had stopped David from avenging himself, and David admitted this was true (vv. 32–34). Abigail admitted that her husband deserved to be judged, but she wanted the Lord to do it, not the king. In fact, she promised that the Lord would judge *all* the enemies of the king.

When David heard the news of Nabal's death, he praised the Lord for avenging him and preventing him from doing it himself. David's concern was the glory of God and the advancement of His kingdom. Abigail certainly must have been pleased to be set free from the yoke of such a wicked man, a man she probably married against her will. David had been so impressed with her character and wisdom that he thought she would make a good queen, so he sent messengers to ask for her hand in marriage. It was an opportunity no woman would refuse, and she submitted to her king and even offered to wash his feet! In marrying Abigail, David not only acquired a good wife, but he also got possession of all of Nabal's wealth and property, which was situated near Hebron where David later established his royal residence (2 Sam. 2:1–4; 5:5). He had already taken Ahinoam as his wife, since she is always named before Abigail (27:3; 30:5; 2 Sam. 2:2). She was the mother of David's first-born son, Amnon, and Abigail bore him Kileab, also named Daniel (1 Chron. 3:1).

—*Be Successful*, page 162, 164

9. What most impressed David about Abigail? Why did he decide to marry her so soon after Nabal's death? Did the inheritance of Nabal's riches likely have anything to do with it? What political advantage might David have

gained in marrying Abigail? What was the spiritual significance behind David's marriage?

From the Commentary

Some students of the Old Testament have tried to prove that the account in chapter 26 is merely an adaptation of the one in chapter 24, but the evidence stands against this interpretation. There are differences in locations (a cave in Engedi; Saul's camp near Hachilah), times (day; night), activities (Saul came to the cave; David went to the camp), David's responses (cutting off part of Saul's robe; taking Saul's spear and water jug), and David's words (spoke only to Saul; spoke to Abner and Saul). This second experience with Saul was certainly more daring on David's part since he was actually in Saul's camp. David's recent experience with Nabal and Abigail had reassured him of his future reign and had taught him a profitable lesson about revenge.

—*Be Successful*, page 165

10. Why might chapter 26 be considered by some to be an adaptation of chapter 24? Is it important that it is a new story? Why or why not? How is the lesson we learn in chapter 26 different from that which we learn in the story described in chapter 24?

Looking Inward

Take a moment to reflect on all that you've explored thus far in this study of 1 Samuel 23—26. Review your notes and answers and think about how each of these things matters in your life today.

Tips for Small Groups: To get the most out of this section, form pairs or trios and have group members take turns answering these questions. Be honest and as open as you can in this discussion, but most of all, be encouraging and supportive of others. Be sensitive to those who are going through particularly difficult times and don't press for people to speak if they're uncomfortable doing so.

11. Describe a time when you lost perspective in a situation and made a poor decision. Why did you lose perspective? What might have helped you maintain a proper perspective? Why is reliance on the Holy Spirit critical when making important decisions? How do you do that?

12. Who are some of the wise older leaders you've learned from? How have they helped you (as Samuel helped David)? What can you do today to prepare yourself to be a wise older leader for someone else someday?

13. David was a diplomatic leader who cared about his followers and provided for them. What are some ways you've provided for others under your care? What are ways you've been provided for by others? How does the way a leader treats you affect your support of that leader?

Going Forward

14. Think of one or two things that you have learned that you'd like to work on in the coming week. Remember that this is all about quality, not quantity. It's better to work on one specific area of life and do it well than to work on many and do poorly (or to be so overwhelmed that you simply don't try).

Do you want to learn how to show mercy as God did to David? Be specific. Go back through 1 Samuel 23—26 and put a star next to the phrase or verse that is most encouraging to you. Consider memorizing this verse.

Real-Life Application Ideas: Samuel played a key role in David's growth as a man and as a leader. This week, seek out the counsel of your church's wisest members. These may be official church elders, or simply believers who have lived a long and full life. Spend time with one or two of these people and engage in conversation about how they grew closer to Christ along their journey. Then look for practical, meaningful ways to honor their lives of faith.

Seeking Help

15. Write a prayer below (or simply pray one in silence), inviting God to work on your mind and heart in those areas you've noted in the Going Forward section. Be honest about your desires and fears.

Notes for Small Groups:

- *Look for ways to put into practice the things you wrote in the Going Forward section. Talk with other group members about your ideas and commit to being accountable to one another.*
- *During the coming week, ask the Holy Spirit to continue to reveal truth to you from what you've read and studied.*
- *Before you start the next lesson, read 1 Samuel 27— 31. For more in-depth lesson preparation, read chapters 11, "Living with the Enemy," and 12, "The King Is Dead!," in* Be Successful.

The King Is Dead!
(1 SAMUEL 27—31)

Before you begin …
- *Pray for the Holy Spirit to reveal truth and wisdom as you go through this lesson.*
- *Read 1 Samuel 27—31. This lesson references chapters 11 and 12 in* Be Successful. *It will be helpful for you to have your Bible and a copy of the commentary available as you work through this lesson.*

Getting Started

From the Commentary

In his more mature years, David heard God say to him, "I will instruct you and teach you in the way you should go; I will guide you with My eye. Do not be like the horse or like the mule" (Ps. 32:8–9 NKJV). The horse is impulsive and rushes heedlessly into the battle, while the mule is stubborn and holds back, and all of us have had both experiences. God doesn't want to deal with us as men deal with animals; He wants to be close to us and guide us with His eye, the way a parent guides a child. When we behold the face of the Lord, we can see His smile or frown and we can discern from His eyes which way He wants us to go.

—Be Successful, page 171

1. What do these chapters say about the experiences of David when he was living without God's intimate guidance? What did David rely on during this season of his life? How is his behavior similar to the way Christians today live their lives when they're far from God?

More to Consider: Read Psalm 13:1–2. What does this passage tell us about David's state of mind during these difficult years of his life? What was David missing in his relationship with God? (See Heb. 6:12.) How is this scene similar to the time when Jesus faced the cross? (John 12:20–33.)

2. Choose one verse or phrase from 1 Samuel 27—31 that stands out to you. This could be something you're intrigued by, something that makes

you uncomfortable, something that puzzles you, something that resonates with you, or just something you want to examine further. Write that here.

Going Deeper

From the Commentary

> God's children must be careful not to yield to despondency. Moses was discouraged over his heavy workload and wanted to die (Num. 11:15), and Elijah ran from the place of duty because of fear and discouragement (1 Kings 19). When we start to look at God through our circumstances instead of looking at our circumstances through God's eyes, we will lose faith, patience, and courage, and the enemy will triumph.
>
> —*Be Successful*, page 172

3. Read Psalm 31:1–5. How do these verses speak to David's despondency? How can they speak to our own seasons of discouragement? How does Proverbs 3:5 speak to the same issues?

From the Commentary

David and his band were kept from fighting with the Philistines, but they still had a battle to fight, this time with the Amalekites, the sworn enemies of the Lord and of the Jews (Ex. 17:8–16; Deut. 25:17). Because Saul had won an incomplete victory over the Amalekites (1 Sam. 15:1–11), they were still free to attack God's people.

Perhaps the Lord permitted this raid on Ziklag to encourage David to get out of enemy territory and go back to Judah where he belonged. The Amalekite leaders knew that David was at Gath and that all attention was focused on the confrontation between Israel and the Philistines. This was a perfect time to retaliate against David for his raids and to pick up some booty as well. Since most of the men were with David, the residents of Ziklag could put up no resistance, and the invaders simply kidnapped the people and took whatever wealth they could find. They burned the city, an act of vengeance on their part but perhaps a message from the Lord that it was time for David to think about returning to Judah.

—*Be Successful*, page 176

4. Review 1 Samuel 30:1–6. How would David and his men have felt after losing their first battle? How did they get back up again after this terrible defeat? In what ways was God merciful to David and his men? Why is this important to David's story?

From the Commentary

When David said to his troops, "This is David's spoil" (30:20), he wasn't claiming the wealth of the Amalekites for himself in a selfish way but only stating that he would see to its distribution. Each of his fighting men received their part and so did the 200 soldiers who were too weary to continue the pursuit. This generosity of David bothered some of the "evil men and troublemakers" in David's band (v. 22 NIV), but David paid them no heed. He politely laid it down as a rule in his army that all the spoils would be divided among all the men, including those who didn't actually fight the enemy. After all, it was the Lord who gave them the victory, so nobody had the right to claim the spoils for himself as if the Lord owed it to him. God was gracious and generous to deliver the enemy into their hands, and they should be gracious and generous to share the wealth with others.

—*Be Successful*, page 178

5. What does the approach David took toward distributing the spoils of war say about his character? About his budding leadership skills? How did his sharing of the spoils help prepare him for the role as king?

From the Commentary

First Samuel opens with the birth of a gifted baby, Samuel, and closes with the death of a guilty man, King Saul. The early chapters cluster around the tabernacle where God spoke to young Samuel, and the closing chapters focus on a forsaken man to whom God refused to speak. Samuel prayed and God defeated the Philistines; Saul sought for God's help but He didn't answer, and the Philistines defeated Israel.

—*Be Successful*, page 183

6. In what ways is 1 Samuel a book about man's king (Saul)? Why did man's king fail? Second Samuel is a book about God's king (David). What are the key differences between the two kings and how they were selected? What does this teach us about God's role in helping us choose good leaders?

From the Commentary

Of all the "night scenes" in the Bible—and there are many of them—the one described in 1 Samuel 28:3–25 is perhaps the strangest and most dramatic. The spirit of a dead man returned to announce the doom of a despairing king who can find no way of escape. Samuel and Saul met for the last time, and it was not a happy meeting.

We have already learned that Samuel was dead (25:1), but the fact is repeated here for perhaps two reasons. First, Israel was in trouble and Samuel wasn't there to rescue them as he had done before (7:7–14), and second, Saul was in trouble and Samuel wasn't there to give him God's counsel. When Samuel was alive, he had told Saul and the people what they needed to do to defeat the Philistines (7:3). However, their faith in God had gradually eroded under the leadership of King Saul, who was now deliberately seeking help from the Evil One. It was Israel's darkest hour, but if God had deserted them, it was only because Saul had first deserted God.

The Philistine army was already mobilizing, and Saul and his army weren't prepared to meet them. When he saw them assembled, he became very frightened and trembled. The Philistines first gathered at Aphek while Israel assembled at Jezreel (29:1). Then the Philistines moved to Jezreel (v. 11) and finally to Shunem (28:4), where they prepared to attack the Israelite army stationed at Mount Gilboa (v. 4; 31:1).

—*Be Successful*, pages 183–184

7. Why did Saul attempt to get in touch with the Lord through dreams? Why did all of Saul's attempts to get an answer from God fail? Did God desert Saul? Why? What does it mean when God deserts someone?

From the Commentary

> Taking the plain meaning of the text in 30:15–19, it seems clear that Samuel did appear to the woman, *but she was shocked when it happened*. Samuel didn't come up from the realm of the dead because she was a good medium but because the Lord willed it to happen. This was not a demon imitating Samuel, or the medium using clever tricks, otherwise the woman wouldn't have been shocked. Her surprised loud cry was evidence that Samuel's sudden appearing was something she didn't expect to happen. She saw the prophet but Saul didn't (vv. 13–14), but Samuel spoke directly to Saul and not through the medium. Samuel was a prophet of God and needed no "mouthpiece" to convey the Lord's message. In fact, verse 21 suggests that the woman was not close to Saul during the time Samuel delivered his message to the king.

Saul had only one question for Samuel: "What shall I do?" The Philistines were ready to attack, Saul was a weak and worried man, and everything he did to ascertain the Lord's will didn't work. "God is departed from me." Seven times in his brief message Samuel used the word "Lord" as he reminded Saul that God had departed from him because he refused to obey God's will. God tore the kingdom from Saul because he hadn't obeyed in the matter of slaying the Amalekites (15:28), and for the first time, Samuel announced that David was the "neighbor" who would inherit the kingdom (28:17). But the direst news of all was that the next day Saul and his sons would be slain in battle and join Samuel in the realm of the dead.

The king was sitting on a couch next to the wall, and when he heard Samuel's words, he fell helpless, full length on the floor. He had wanted a message from the Lord, but when it came, it wasn't the message he wanted to hear. He was trembling with fear at hearing the announcement of his death, and he was weak from fasting. Why would a general fast before a strategic battle? Was Saul trying to buy help from the Lord as he had done once before (14:28)? Some authorities believe that mediums required people to fast before they came to a séance, so perhaps Saul had that in mind.

—*Be Successful*, pages 185–186

8. Review 1 Samuel 30:15–25. What do these verses reveal about Saul's state near the end of his life? Did he feel regret over his abandonment of God? Why or why not? What role did fear play in his attempt to get God's help?

More to Consider: The medium shifted into a motherly role and begged the king to eat something. He had a dangerous journey ahead of him back to his camp, and the next day he had to direct his troops in the battle against the Philistines. As he had foolishly done before, Saul tried to "play the man" and appear the hero, substituting bravado for sanity, but the pleas of the medium and Saul's men prevailed. The woman must have been fairly well-to-do to have a fattened calf readily available, because this was the diet of the wealthy and a rare delicacy for the common people. Indeed, it was a meal fit for a king, but it was also his "last supper" before leaving this life. How does the final statement in the chapter remind us of Judas? (See John 13:30.)

From the Commentary

Saul's military record is summarized in 1 Samuel 14:47–48. It's a commendable record that presents Saul as a conquering general and a national hero. He began his career as a great success; after all, the people did sing, "Saul has slain his thousands." It was after his failure to destroy the Amalekites that Saul began to go downhill. When David came on the scene, Saul's envy of the young man's success so obsessed him that the king became paranoid and dangerous.

—*Be Successful*, page 187

9. Review 1 Samuel 31:1–10 and 1 Chronicles 10. How did envy lead to Saul's downfall? How would his reign have been different if he'd practiced humility? What was the ultimate result of his pride and disobedience? What does Saul's story tell us about the importance of being humble?

From the Commentary

While the Philistines were making merry over defeating Israel and humiliating Saul and his sons, the men of Jabesh Gilead heard about the tragedy and came to the rescue. King Saul's first great victory had been the delivering of Jabesh Gilead from the Ammonites (1 Sam.

11:1–11), so the people of the city felt an obligation to vindicate Saul's memory. All of their valiant men traveled fifteen to twenty miles at night to the city of Bethshan and took possession of the four mutilated and decaying bodies. In order to make this trip, they had to cross the Jordan River and go through enemy territory. Saul hadn't been a spiritual leader, but he was a courageous leader and the first king of Israel. Even if we can't respect the man, we must show respect for the office.

The men risked their lives a second time and carried the bodies to Jabesh Gilead. There they burned the bodies to remove the mutilated and decayed flesh, and they left the bones for burial. They didn't cremate the bodies, because cremation wasn't a Jewish practice. In times of emergency, the Jews would burn corpses that were so mutilated and decayed they couldn't be properly washed and anointed for burial, and then they would give honorable burial to the bones. After the people of Jabesh Gilead buried the bones, they fasted for seven days. It was their tribute to Saul and his sons.

Saul had often held court under a tree in Ramah (22:6), and now he was buried with three of his sons under a tree near Jabesh Gilead. Later, David disinterred the bones of Saul and Jonathan and had them buried in their family's tomb in Benjamin (2 Sam. 21:13–14).

—*Be Successful*, pages 189–190

10. Why did the people pay tribute to Saul? What good things had he done for the Israelites? How is his story ultimately a story of a man who started out strong and lost his way? What could have helped him stay on track in his relationship with God?

Looking Inward

Take a moment to reflect on all that you've explored thus far in this study of 1 Samuel 27—31. Review your notes and answers and think about how each of these things matters in your life today.

> *Tips for Small Groups: To get the most out of this section, form pairs or trios and have group members take turns answering these questions. Be honest and as open as you can in this discussion, but most of all, be encouraging and supportive of others. Be sensitive to those who are going through particularly difficult times and don't press for people to speak if they're uncomfortable doing so.*

11. Describe a time when you felt despondent or discouraged. Were you quick to seek God's guidance during this time? Was it easy to trust that God was still in control? Explain. How can David's psalms help you endure the difficult times?

12. Have you ever felt like Saul did when God deserted him? Describe the situation that led to that feeling. Did God actually desert you, or did you move away from God? How can you tell the difference?

13. What are some ways humility has helped you in your relationship with God? With others? What's the difference between being humble and being spineless? How has God taught you about humility?

Going Forward

14. Think of one or two things that you have learned that you'd like to work on in the coming week. Remember that this is all about quality, not quantity. It's better to work on one specific area of life and do it well than to work on many and do poorly (or to be so overwhelmed that you simply don't try).

Do you want to talk with God about feelings of discouragement? Be specific. Go back through 1 Samuel 27—31 and put a star next to the phrase or verse that is most encouraging to you. Consider memorizing this verse.

Real-Life Application Ideas: Saul didn't do a very good job of listening to God after his first few years as king. This week, avoid his fate by spending lots of time in prayer, listening for God's direction in all areas of your life. Choose a specific theme for each day (family, friends, work, worship, service, etc.) and focus on that theme in your prayer time.

Seeking Help

15. Write a prayer below (or simply pray one in silence), inviting God to work on your mind and heart in those areas you've noted in the Going Forward section. Be honest about your desires and fears.

Notes for Small Groups:

- *Look for ways to put into practice the things you wrote in the Going Forward section. Talk with other group members about your ideas and commit to being accountable to one another.*
- *During the coming week, ask the Holy Spirit to continue to reveal truth to you from what you've read and studied.*

Summary and Review

Notes for Small Groups: This session is a summary and review of this book. Because of that, it is shorter than the previous lessons. If you are using this in a small-group setting, consider combining this lesson with a time of fellowship or a shared meal.

Before you begin …
- *Pray for the Holy Spirit to reveal truth and wisdom as you go through this lesson.*
- *Briefly review the notes you made in the previous sessions. You will refer back to previous sections throughout this bonus lesson.*

Looking Back

1. Over the past eight lessons, you've examined 1 Samuel. What expectations did you bring to this study? In what ways were those expectations met?

2. What is the most significant personal discovery you've made from this study?

3. What surprised you most about 1 Samuel? What, if anything, troubled you?

Progress Report

4. Take a few moments to review the Going Forward sections of the previous lessons. How would you rate your progress for each of the things you chose to work on? What adjustments, if any, do you need to make to continue on the path toward spiritual maturity?

5. In what ways have you grown closer to Christ during this study? Take a moment to celebrate those things. Then think of areas where you feel you still need to grow and note those here. Make plans to revisit this study in a few weeks to review your growing faith.

Things to Pray About

6. First Samuel is a book about what it means to be successful in God's eyes. As you reflect on this, ask God to show you how to apply the lessons in the book to your own life of faith.

7. The messages in 1 Samuel include character, trust, dealing with pride, overcoming trials, obeying God, and listening for God's voice. Spend time praying for each of these topics.

8. Whether you've been studying this in a small group or on your own, there are many other Christians working through the very same issues you discovered when examining 1 Samuel. Take time to pray for each of them, that God would reveal truth, that the Holy Spirit would guide you, and that each person might grow in spiritual maturity according to God's will.

A Blessing of Encouragement

Studying the Bible is one of the best ways to learn how to be more like Christ. Thanks for taking this step. In closing, let this blessing precede you and follow you into the next week while you continue to marinate in God's Word:

May God light your path to greater understanding as you review the truths found in 1 Samuel and consider how they can help you grow closer to Christ.

FIND TRUE SUCCESS
THROUGH A LIFE OF INTEGRITY AND CHARACTER

Part of Dr. Warren W. Wiersbe's bestselling "BE" commentary series, *BE Successful* has now been updated with study questions and a new introduction by Ken Baugh. A respected pastor and Bible teacher, Dr. Wiersbe journeys through the book of 1 Samuel to uncover how God defines success. This guide examines the life of King David and shares how we can find true success through our character, conduct, and lifestyle. You will be inspired to pursue your goals and encouraged to make the race just as important as the finish line.

David C Cook

transforming lives together